BRADSHAW'S GUIDES

Volume Eleven: Surrey & Sussex Railways

Simon Jeffs

Series Editor John Christopher

AMBERLEY

About this book

This book is intended to encourage the reader to explore many aspects of railway travel since Bradshaw's times. Through his account and the supportive images and information, it describes the history of the railways, their engineering works, architecture and some of the many changes that have occurred over the years. Hopefully it will encourage you to delve a little deeper when exploring the history of the railways, but please note that public access and photography is sometimes restricted for reasons of safety and security.

Left: George Bradshaw. Although he died in 1853, the guide books that bore his name continued to be printed and will forever be known as 'Bradshaw's Guides'.

First published 2014

Amberley Publishing
The Hill, Stroud
Gloucestershire, GL5 4EP

www.amberley-books.com

Copyright © Simon Jeffs & John Christopher, 2014

The right of Simon Jeffs and John Christopher to be identified as the Authors of this work has been asserted in accordance with the Copyrights, Designs and Patents Act 1988.

ISBN 978 1 4456 4040 2 (print)
ISBN 978 1 4456 4073 0 (ebook)

British Library Cataloguing in Publication Data.
A catalogue record for this book is available from the British Library.

Typeset in 9.5pt on 12pt Celeste.
Typesetting by Amberley Publishing.
Printed in the UK.

Surrey and Sussex Railways

This is the eleventh volume in this series of books based on *Bradshaw's Descriptive Railway Hand-Book of Great Britain and Ireland,* which was originally published in 1863.

George Bradshaw was born in 1801 and died at the age of fifty-two in 1853. By chance he lived at a time of an unprecedented transport revolution. The railway engineers drove the iron roads, with their cuttings, embankments and tunnels, through a predominantly rural landscape to lay the foundations of the nineteenth-century industrial powerhouse that has shaped the way we live today. It is fair to say that the railways are the Victorians' greatest legacy to the twentieth and twenty-first centuries. They shrank space and time. Before their coming different parts of the country had existed in local time based on the position of the sun, with Bristol, for example, running ten minutes behind London. The railways changed all when they introduced synchronised railway time. The presence of the railways defined the shape and development of many of our towns and cities, they altered the distribution of the population and forever changed the fundamental patterns of our lives. For many millions of Britons the daily business of where they live and work, and travel between the two, is defined by the network of iron rails laid down by the nineteenth-century railway engineers and an anonymous army of railway navvies.

Below: 1920s map of Sussex and Surrey railway lines, with those covered by Bradshaw in red. *(CMcC)*

Above: Survivors of LBSCR days in the entrance to Victoria station. Produced in ceramic tiles, these maps show the whole system, on the left, the suburban lines, on the right. *(JC)*

The timing of the publication of Bradshaw's guidebooks is interesting. This particular account is taken from the 1863 edition of the handbook although, for practical reasons, it must have been written slightly earlier, probably between 1860 and 1862. By this stage the railways had lost their pioneering status, and with the heady days of the railway mania of the 1840s over, they were settling into the daily business of transporting people and goods. It was also by this time that rail travel had become sufficiently commonplace to create a market for Bradshaw's guides.

As a young man George Bradshaw had been apprenticed to an engraver in Manchester in 1820, and after a spell in Belfast he returned to Manchester to set up his own business as an engraver and printer specialising principally in maps. In October 1839 he produced the world's first compilation of railway timetables. Entitled *Bradshaw's Railway Time Tables and Assistant to Railway Travelling*, the slender cloth-bound volume sold for sixpence. By 1840 the title had changed to *Bradshaw's Railway Companion* and the price doubled to one shilling. It then evolved into a monthly publication with the price reduced to the original and more affordable sixpence.

Although George Bradshaw died in 1852, the company continued to produce the monthly guides and in 1863 it launched Bradshaw's *Descriptive Railway Hand-Book of Great Britain and Ireland* (which forms the basis of this series of books). It was originally published in four sections as proper guidebooks without any of the timetable information of the monthly publications. Universally referred to as *Bradshaw's Guide*, it is this guidebook that features in Michael Portillo's *Great British Railway Journeys*, and as a result of its exposure to a new audience the book found itself catapulted into the best seller list almost 150 years after it was originally published.

Without a doubt, the *Bradshaw* guides were invaluable in their time and they provide the modern-day reader with a fascinating insight into the mid-Victorian rail traveller's experience. In 1865 *Punch* had praised Bradshaw's publications, stating that 'seldom has the gigantic intellect of man been employed upon a work of greater utility'. Having said that, the usual facsimile editions available nowadays don't make especially easy reading with their columns of close-set type. There are scarcely any illustrations for a start, and attempts to trace linear journeys from A to B can be difficult. That's where this volume of illustrated *Bradshaw's Guides* comes into its own. In the first section it takes the traveller via the London, Brighton & South Coast Railway (LBSCR) on the mainline from the capital due south to Brighton. The second section looks at the lines extending in either dirction from Brighton following the south coast, heading westwards to Chichester on the Portsmouth line, and eastwards via the Brighton to Lewes branch and continuing as far as Hastings. Winchelsea and Rye are reached from the Kent side on the line coming down from Ashford. The remaining lines within Surrey include the London & South Western Railway's (LSWR) rails into East Surrey and over the river on the loop into Middlesex, plus branches connecting Wimbledon with Croydon and Epsom, and also Wimbledon, Epsom and Leatherhead. The Guildford to Alton branch takes in the western extreme of Surrey as far as Farnham, while the Reading, Guildford and Reigate branch reaches up into the north-western corner of the county. As for Sussex, those parts not covered in the first two sections are represented in 'Sussex Branch Lines', including from Three Bridges to Horsham and Petworth as well as East Grinstead, plus Haywards Heath to Newhaven, Lewes to Uckfield, and also the Tunbridge Wells to St Leonards line running down the eastern side.

In some instances Bradshaw's descriptions of locations have been rearranged as to fit with the linear journeys being described. The illustrations showing scenes from Victorian times are juxtaposed with new photographs of many of the locations as they are today, and accompanied by information from local rail historian Simon Jeffs to provide greater background detail on the railways and the places on the route.

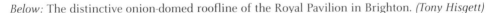

Below: The distinctive onion-domed roofline of the Royal Pavilion in Brighton. *(Tony Hisgett)*

Above: Glynde, a 2-2-2 passenger express loco built for the London Brighton & South Coast Railway by Robert Stephenson & Co. *(Tony Hisgett)*

Left: Postcard view of the Central Station in Brighton, *c.* 1903. *(CMcC)*

Left: Bradshaw's guidebooks played a considerable part in bringing holidaymakers and day-trippers to the seaside. These bathing machines were mobile changing huts, enabling both sexes to dip in the briney with their modesty intact. *(LoC)*

London to Brighton

SUSSEX

One of the Southern Counties, is varied by the inequalities of the Downs and by intervening valleys, to which the wooded scenery and pasture land give a rural and a rich diversity of appearance. It belongs to the chalk formation, and has some high ranges of downs and hills. The north is occupied by Wealden formation, covering 420,000 acres, and the south by the chalk formation. On the coast are marshes and alluvial lands, and on the west coast it is much indented by, at others it runs out into, bold cliffs.

This county is celebrated for its breed of sheep, which are fed on the South Downs, the name by which they are distinguished. This, and the adjoining counties of Hants and Surrey, were by the Romans denominated Belgae, from the circumstance of their being inhabited by a people called Belgians, who supplanted the British Celts.

The railway communication of the county of Sussex is supplied by the London, Brighton, & South Coast Railway Company. The London and Brighton main line, commencing at the London Bridge Terminus, proceeds past Sydenham and Croydon to Reigate, thence enters the county of Sussex at Crawley, and passes due South to Brighton, having branch lines extending along the coast to Lewes and Hastings, and Newhaven to the north, and to Shoreham, Worthing, Arundel, Chichester, Havant, and Portsmouth on the south.

The London & Brighton Railway is 50 ½ miles in length, and traverses a considerable portion of the counties of Surrey and Sussex.

The Brighton Company was the first to commence running excursion trains, which are now provided by most of the other companies throughout the United Kingdom, as affording a profitable source of revenue to the companies, and being the means of 'popularising' the towns, localities, and scenery in connection with the respective lines.

Railways may now be considered as accelerators of pleasure as well as of business, bringing as they do the most favourite watering places along the coast within the compass of a brief and agreeable journey. Of these mediums of transit, we know of few more inviting to the tourist than the one we are about to describe, passing as it does, through a succession of the most varied and diversified scenery, fraught with a host of welcome associations, and terminating at a sea-side town, which, fashion in pursuit of pleasure has justly selected for a marine residence.

LONDON TO CROYDON

The London terminus [London Bridge station] of the Brighton Railway, though approached by the same line as the South Eastern Railway, is a distinct building, occupying a considerable place to the south, at the right hand or furthest corner of the fabric, and embraces in its arrangements everything calculated to promote the convenience of the passengers, and all that can contribute to their security.

So entangled is the mighty maze of London with its suburbs, that on emerging from the station it is some time before we entirely lose sight of its multifarious

London Bridge station
Opened as the terminus of the
London to Greenwich Railway in
December 1836, this was a 'joint'
station, accommodating the
LBSCR and South Eastern
Railway in Bradshaw's time.
Recently it has been in the
throes of redevelopment to
accommodate an enhanced
Thameslink service.
'Networker' 465242
waits to depart in
October 2012.
(Simon Jeffs)

LONDON BRIDGE STATION.

465242

Victoria station

Although both the LBSCR and LCDR had commenced using Victoria for passenger services from 1860, Bradshaw doesn't mention it and directs travellers to London Bridge.

Above and right: Pullman trains became a feature at Victoria from 1881 until 1972 when both the Golden Arrow and Brighton Belle, shown here, passed into history. *(John Scrace/JC)*

Right: Since 1958, traffic from Gatwick Airport has assumed ever greater importance at Victoria, particularly with the advent of budget airlines, and also the withdrawal of all boat trains from London once the Eurostar service through the Channel Tunnel commenced in 1994. The Gatwick Express service has run non-stop to the airport station since 1984. *(Simon Jeffs)*

Above: LBSCR official postcard of the Brighton Pullman Limited, *c.* 1905. The Pullman carriages established unprecedented levels of comfort for rail travellers. *(CMcC)*

Below: The modern station building at Forest Hill. The original was opened by the London & Croydon Railway in 1839 as Dartford Arms, and used by both the LBSCR and SCR. Although extremely busy it is cursed with one of the ugliest, inadequate stations on the line. *(Simon Jeffs)*

characteristics; we seem, Asmodeus-like, to be fleeting over the habitations of a dense and crowded district. The first part of the line to New Cross is carried over arches, and continues so for some time, passing by a viaduct over market gardens, as far as the Greenwich Junction, and then turns off towards New Cross, where the Company has a large depot for repairing locomotives. Immediately the line emerges from the streets and houses that obstruct the view, and the Crystal Palace at Sydenham, sparkling in the distance, appears in sight.

NEW CROSS
A telegraph station.

From this station the line passes through cuttings that exclude all view of the country; the passengers, however, cannot fail to admire the ingenuity with which the declivities on each side have been converted into flower and kitchen gardens. Emerging from tins cutting a wide and extensive prospect of undulating ground is opened on both sides. To the east appears a succession of gardens; to the west, a glimpse of the cemetery at Nunhead is obtained. Sydenham and Norwood appear next in succession, studded with white villas, and on every side a range of wooded and picturesque scenery is unfolded to the view.

FOREST HILL
A telegraph station.

To the right we see Dulwich, famous for the picture gallery, in 'Dulwich, or God's Gift, College, founded by Edward Alleyne, the Player, the Proteus, for shape, and the Roscius, for tongue.' Built in 1619, supported by an income of £8,637 arising from landed property and bequests, and which is open for view to the public by ticket. To the left lies the village of Sydenham, celebrated for its beauty and salubrity, and shortly after we reach the station at

SYDENHAM
A telegraph station. Hotel – Royal.
Omnibuses from Norwood to all parts of London every quarter of an hour.
Post Office at the Crystal Palace. Money Order Office at Upper Norwood.

This station is situated in the midst of most beautiful scenery and in view of the Crystal Palace. A small branch railway conveys passengers from the station to the palace, from which a continuation of the same railway will convey them on to Croydon to re-join the main line, if their destination be onwards. Whether the reader be going on a visit to the palace or merely passing it *en route* to a more distant station, the view of the gleaming dome and marvellous structure, which crowns the breezy heights of Sydenham, will always excite his wonder and admiration.

The Crystal Palace

This magnificent cast-iron and plate-glass building, *below*, was first erected in Hyde Park, London, England, to house the Great Exhibition of 1851. Designed by Sir Joseph Paxton, it was was 1,851 feet long, with an interior height of 128 feet. At the time, it contained the largest amount of glass ever seen, thus is was dubbed as the 'Crystal Palace' by *Punch*. The exhibition closed after six months and with funding from a consortium of businessmen (two of them board members of the LBSCR), it was rebuilt in an enlarged form on Penge Common next to Sydenham Hill.

Left: It was served by two stations. The first, later known as Low Level, was opened in 1854 by the West End of London & Crystal Palace Railway, with trains provided by the LBSCR. It is now the only one as the High Level station closed in 1954. *(Simon Jeffs)*

CRYSTAL PALACE

A telegraph station.

Situated about half way between Sydenham and Anerley station, on the right side of the railway from London to Croydon, the site of the Crystal Palace on the summit of Penge Park, is one of the most beautiful in the world. Standing on the brow of the hill, some two hundred feet above the valley through which the railway passes, the building is visible for many miles in every direction. But when the train approaches the spot where the brilliant and fairy fabric, in the midst of the most enchanting scenery, is revealed suddenly to the eye, the impression produced elicits our warmest admiration. The models of the diluvian and antediluvian extinct animals, the Irish elk with its magnificently branching antlers, the two Ignanodons, the Megalosaurus, etc., etc., in the foreground among the Geological Islands and Lakes; the cascades and terraces, the luxuriant foliage, flower-beds and fountains, ascending up to the splendid and unrivalled fabric of glass which rears its radiant and glittering bulk upon the Surrey hill, form a *coup d'oeil* of wonderful beauty, magnificence, and grandeur, the view of which we may envy the Brighton Railway traveller who enjoys the sight daily, in virtue of his season ticket.

Anyone who appreciates the beautiful will always feel gratified even with a passing view; but every person who can spare the time should visit it on a fete day.

Excursion trains to and from London Bridge afford every facility. The building, the grounds or park, the salubrity of the air, the waterworks, the garden inside and out, the fine art courts and collections, form a combination of attractions unsurpassed in any country.

The visitor from London is conveyed to the station of the Crystal Palace in twenty minutes. On emerging from the train he ascends the flight of stairs in the south wing and reaches the centre nave or great transept in a few moments, and immediately beholds that unrivalled view which we all admire with feelings of pride and satisfaction as the most wonderful work human hands and mind have yet achieved.

The whole of the sides of the nave and the divisions on either side are lined with plants and trees from every clime, interspersed with statues and works of art, and embellished with beautiful fountains in the centre. The great transept, with its trees and flowers and fountains divides the nave into two equal parts – the northern division dedicated to art, and the southern to commerce, or to the industrial display of the manufactures of the United Kingdom, which, by the way, under injudicious management is becoming not only less attractive than formerly, but quite contemptible. The transept has the appearance of an immense conservatory, embellished with the finest and rarest models and *chefs d'oeuvres* of ancient and modem statuary. This series of courts represents and illustrates the architecture of ancient art.

The **Pompeian Court** is the exact facsimile of the interior of a building discovered in the ruins of Pompeii. Mosaic pavements and walls, divided into compartments, in which mythological subjects are beautifully painted.

The **Egyptian Court** is highly suggestive of the grand and massive character of Egyptian architecture and its lion-faced Sphinxes, its solemn heads of colossal women, its gigantic figures, and its walls covered with hieroglyphics.

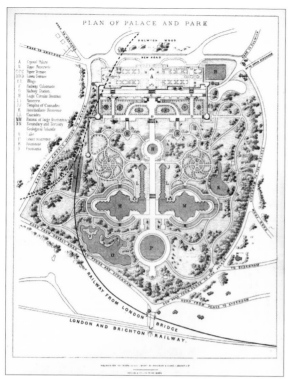

PLAN OF PALACE AND PARK

Left: A plan of the park showing the Crystal Palace at the top. It was destroyed by fire on 30 November 1936. The grounds and gardens have survived and the site bears the 719-foot BBC TV Transmitter. When built in 1956, this mast was the tallest structure in the UK and has only been recently exceeded by One Canada Square at Canary Wharf and the Shard. The sweeping steps to the Palace still stand, guarded by sphinxes, overleaf, and there is a huge bust of Joseph Paxton standing in the park, close to the National Sports Centre and stadium. *(Simon Jeffs)*

The **Greek Court**, containing copies of unrivalled works of sculpture, groups of great beauty, and specimens of perfect architecture.

The **Roman Court**, richly stored with Roman sculpture, models, and curious gems.

The **Alhambra Court**, representing several courts of the *famous palace* of the Moorish Kings of Granada, the Court of Lions, and Hall of Justice.

The **Assyrian and Nineveh Court**, displaying the wonders of Nineveh, with its colossal divinities, Rhea, and the gigantic Sphinxes, its eagle- winged and human-headed hulls, and its cuneiform hieroglyphics. And then on the opposite side are the several courts, in which are given illustrations of the Byzantine, Mediaeval, and Renaissance styles of architecture, including models of the French, English. German, and Italian schools, each court being complete in itself, and entered by a characteristic doorway.

Modern Picture Gallery – In this extensive space will be found one of the best lighted and most spacious galleries of modern pictures to he found in England, These works of art have been contributed by proprietors, and also by artists, and many of them are deposited here for sale. Thus this portion of the building combines the attractions of private collections and public exhibitions, with the additional advantage, that only the best works of art are accepted for exhibition.

On leaving the central transept the visitor descends a flight of granite steps leading to the Upper Terrace, which extends within the two advancing wings of the palace, and commands a splendid view of the gardens, and of the whole country beyond the railway, to the summit of the Surrey hills. The Terrace Garden is adorned with a central circular basin, throwing out a *Jet d'Eau*, besides others of an elliptical shape. At the extremity of each wing there is a tower in the form of a Greek Cross, which have each on their summit a tank, containing 924 tons of water, to be distributed for any

Above: The Victorians were fascinated by the newly discovered dinosaur fossils and the sculptor Benjamin Waterhouse Hawkins built thirty-three life-size models using iron skeletal frames covered by a combination of brick and cement. They are still there in the Park. *(Simon Jeffs)*

Above: This guardian sphinx remains as a relic of Crystal Palace's former glories. *(Simon Jeffs)*

purposes throughout the building. [The guide is incorrect as the towers, designed by Brunel, were cylindrical.] The high towers, of which there are two, one at each end of the building, have been erected for the purpose of carrying the tanks that supply the fountains in the lower basin, and are, with the exception of the tank and stays, constructed of cast-iron.

Flights of steps lead to the Italian and Flower Garden and Terrace below, and to a series of basins and caves, receiving fountains, and waterfalls, containing six times the amount of water thrown up by the Grand Eaux at Versailles.

Along the great walk the water of the upper basin flows down in a series of cascades, until it falls into an open colonnade, and then rushes into falls on each side of the walk, half a mile in length, which supply numerous other fountains.

On ordinary occasions the basins and fountains give life and freshness to the garden, hut on fete days the vast waters are unloosed, and rushing upwards in a thousand streams or dashing over the colonnades, make the whole garden ring with their tumultuous murmurings, producing a magnificent effect, a splendid brilliancy in the sunbeam, joined to the fragrance and freshness of the flowers, of which few can form a conception who have not witnessed it. One of the most curious features of the Palace is the Geological Islands, and the specimens of tire extinct animals, life-like gigantic models of which are distributed over the islands and lakes.

There is a splendid Refreshment Room for the first class visitors, where parties can have hot dinners served in first-rate style, at not unreasonable prices.

For the convenience of the inhabitants of Belgravia and the west end of London, a line has been formed to run from Victoria Station, Chelsea, via Battersea, New Wandsworth, Balham, Steatham, at which there is a tunnel, Lower Norwood, and Gipsey Hill, to the Crystal Palace. The scenery along the line is remarkable for its fertility and beauty. It joins the main line from London Bridge at Norwood Junction, a little below the Palace.

Resuming our seats in the train we arrive at Anerley Station.

NORWOOD, UPPER

Distance from station, 1 1/2 mile. A telegraph station,

Hotels – Beulah Spa, Royal Albert, Royal Crystal Palace. Money Order Office.

Norwood is situated on the sides and summit of a considerable eminence, in a most salubrious spot, surrounded with beautiful views of hill and dale, and woodland scenery and of all the most picturesque sites in the two counties of Kent and Surrey. The view, from Upper Norwood, of the west-end of London presents a superb panorama. When the Beulah Spa of Norwood was in its zenith of fame and celebrity, the gipsies were greatly petted by the visitors, but they disappeared with the decline of the Spa, and now rarely visit the neighbourhood. Norwood lies near the Croydon Railway, of which there is a station in the vicinity. The train passes through a lovely and picturesque country.

Early railways in the area: The Surrey Iron Railway, *right*, was a horse-drawn railway from Wandsworth, which in 1805 was extended to Merstham. The London & Croydon Railway opened between London Bridge and West Croydon in 1839, using much of the route of the Croydon Canal, which had branched off the Grand Surrey Canal at Deptford, *below. (CMcC)*

Croydon
The arrival of the railways and other communication advances in the nineteenth century led to a twenty-three-fold increase in Croydon's population between 1801 and 1901. The major station in Croydon is now East Croydon, *left. (Simon Jeffs)*
The older station, West Croydon, *below,* remains very busy and is adjacent to the town's main bus station. *(Graham Feakins)*

Left: A fine postcard showing the men of the Croydon Corporation Tramways band. *(CMcC)*

CROYDON

Population, 28,325. Distance from station, 1 mile.

A telegraph station. Hotels – Greyhound, Crown.

Market Days – Thursday and Saturday. Fairs – July 6th and October 2nd.

Money Order Office. Bankers – London and County Bank; Chasemore and Robinson.

The town of Croydon derives its name from croie, chalk, and *dune*, or hill, from which latter term we obtain our English word 'downs' as signifying an extensive range of hills. It is situated in the midst of a beautiful country, and is a place of considerable antiquity. It consists of one principal street, more than a mile in length, and a number of smaller ones. The church is a noble building, and has a lofty square tower adorned with pinnacles. The Archbishops of Canterbury, for several centuries, made the old manor house, near the church, their occasional residence. A mile and a half from the town is Addiscombe, at which there is a college for the education of cadets for the service of the East India Company.

At this point there are four distinct lines of rails, an arrangement which insures the safety of travellers at the station, the main line being left free for the passage of any express or special train, and the current train turned off into what are technically termed the 'sidings.'

The line now passes through a fine open country, and shortly reaches the junction of the Epsom Branch of the Croydon Railway. [*See page 81.*] After leaving Croydon we pass through a short cutting, and emerge upon an embankment upwards of two miles long, which affords delightful views of the surrounding scenery; and at the distance of about miles from Croydon, arrive at the station of ...

Above: The Spencer airship at Croydon, *c.* 1908. C. G. Spencer & Sons – five of the family were aeronauts – had a balloon shed at Crystal Palace which was a popular site for balloon ascents. *(CMcC)*

Redhill

A major junction between the North-South London–Brighton line and East-West Reading–Tonbridge line, once part of the SER's main route to Dover and the continent. The name derives from the red sandstone through which the Tonbridge branch was constructed and the LBSCR's 'Quarry Line', avoiding Redhill, was tunnelled in 1899. *(John Scrace) Below left:* Platform 3 of the station retains many buildings from the 1858 rebuild. *(Simon Jeffs) Below right:* Beneath Reigate the Barons Cave is all that remains of the castle. It is open to the public. *(Peter Burgess)*

CATERHAM JUNCTION
A telegraph station.

This place commands a fine view of several mansions and seats in the surrounding parks. That of *Selsdon Park*, the property of G. R. Smith, Esq.; of *Purley House*, the property of E. B. Kemble, Esq, once the residence of John Home Tooke; and *Sandershead Place*, the habitation of George Clise, Esq.

Caterham Branch – see page 81

Proceeding on our way to the south the train passes close to the village of **Chipstead**, the church of which, dedicated to St Margaret, is of Norman style, and of considerable antiquity. Sir Edward Banks, the well-known contractor and builder of the London, Southwark and Waterloo Bridges, is buried in this quiet and rural churchyard, near the scenes of his early career, where he commenced life in the neighbourhood as a labourer. *The Oaks* (2 miles), Lord Derby.

Proceeding on, some high grounds now intercept our view, until the line enters the Merstham tunnel, rather more than a mile, long, and in some parts nearly 190 feet below the surface. The transition from the gloomy darkness of the tunnel to the day light we had temporarily forsaken is certainly agreeable, and we are rewarded on emerging by a pretty view of the little village of Merstham, and the adjacent country.

After passing Merstham station, which is a minor one, we obtain a fine view of *Gatton* and its picturesque park, the property of the Dowager Countess of Warwick, and famous before the Reform Bill as haying returned two members to parliament, with a population of a hundred persons, living in scarcely two dozen houses. Half a mile further on, an embankment 20 feet high brings us to

REIGATE or RED HILL
This station is reciprocally used by both the Brighton and Dover trains, the latter diverging to the east, and we at once enter the valley of Holmesdale. The hills to the north seclude both the villages of Hatfield and Bletchingly. Leaving Reigate to the right, we proceed across the embankment formed by Earl's Wood, from which a succession of beautiful varied scenery hires the eye, Leith Hill, Box Hill, and the eminences round Dorking may be clearly discerned.

REIGATE (RED HILL)
A telegraph station. Hotel – Railway Hotel. Money Order Office at Reigate.

On alighting at this station the traveller will find himself in the midst of the celebrated valley of Holmesdale, surrounded on all sides by elevated hills. To the north appears the great chalk range, bearing a rugged and abrupt front, broken into precipitous cliffs, or crowned with undulating heights. To the south is seen the sand-stone ridge, with the celebrated mount of coloured stone, known as 'Red Hill'.

Reigate

Yet another dormitory for London-bound commuters, although Gatwick Airport to the south also provides employment, Reigate grew up below its twelfth-century castle, of which nothing remains above ground, although a mock medieval gateway was built on its ruins. Reigate retains a direct service to London for its heavy commuter traffic, the line was electrified in July 1932. *(Colin Scott-Morton)*

Horley

Left: Horley station in 1870 before quadrupling of the lines, and, *below*, as it looked in 2012. *(Laurel Arnison)* The building on the overbridge shows 1905 as the date of the quadrupling. There was an international airport at Croydon, but this closed in the 1950s to be replaced by Heathrow and Gatwick. The station now serving Gatwick originally opened in 1891 as Gatwick Racecourse but was rebuilt and reopened in 1958. *(Simon Jeffs)*

REIGATE TOWN

Population, 9,975. Distance from station ½ mile. A telegraph station.

Hotels – White Hart, and Swan. Post Horses, Flys, etc., at the station and hotels.

Market Days – Tuesdays. Fairs – Whit-Monday and December 9th.

Money Order Office. Bankers – London & County Joint Stock Banking Company.

Reigate, situated near the River Mole, in the valley of Holmesdale, at the foot of the ridge of chalk hills which traverse the county from east to west, consists of a main street of well-built houses, crossed at the eastern end by the Old Brighton Road, which, for upwards of a mile out of town, is adorned by the detached residences of the gentry. The houses of the lower classes present models of architecture, and are beautifully decorated with imbricated tiles of various patterns, a style of cottage ornament characteristic of this part of the country. The church stands on a gentle eminence east of the town, and is a spacious structure of almost every period of Gothic architecture, some parts of which are extremely beautiful. From the summit of Park Hill an extensive view is obtained of the Wealds of Surrey and Sussex; and that of Reigate, with the priory and its park, is of singular beauty. On the north side of the town, in the principal street, was situated the castle, some few traces of which are yet visible. It was one of the principal seats of the powerful earls of Warwick and Surrey; and here the insurgent barons are reported to have held frequent meetings, preceding the celebrated Congress of Runnymeade. There is a long passage under the castle leading into a vaulted room, called the Baron's cave, which is said to have been used by the barons as a hiding-place for arms. The church has a few curious and ancient tombs.

For the section of the Reigate to Reading branch within Surrey see page 81.

HORLEY

Distance from station, ¾ mile. A telegraph station. Hotel – King's Head.

Horley was once famous for its iron works. It has traces of an old castle. The church is a fine edifice, and contains some handsome monuments.

From the Horley station the line begins for some time rising, and the view on every side continues, as before, uninterrupted. Four miles beyond, the railway passes over the boundary line into the county of Sussex, and arrives at

THREE BRIDGES

A telegraph station.

This station is the junction point of the Horsham Branch – see page 89.
Three Bridges to East Grinstead Branch – see page 91.

Three Bridges

Above: Three Bridges in 1890. This was the junction for the lines to Horsham and on the Petworth (later Arundel and Littlehampton) and the East Grinstead (later Tunbridge Wells) lines, which opened in 1848 and 1855, respectively. The current station, *top left,* dates from the 1907 quadrupling. Photographed in 2012. *(Laurel Arnison)* The line to East Grinstead closed in 1967, but Three Bridges remains a major railway centre, with a massive servicing depot for the new Thameslink Class 700 EMUs under construction. Adjacent is the Regional Operating Centre, *left,* which is one of thirteen sites opening around the UK that will control all rail signalling and operations. *(Simon Jeffs)*

Burgess Hill

Since electrification in 1933, the main line has acted as a conduit for commuters, primarily to London, but with significant flows to Brighton, Gatwick Airport and Croydon.
Left: Burgess Hill in 1890.

THREE BRIDGES TO HAYWARD'S HEATH

The line now passes over an embankment of considerable length, and the railway thence commences a descent. Passing through a series of cuttings, we enter the Balcombe tunnel, the second of the great tunnels along the line, soon after emerging from which we arrive at the Balcombe station.

The line proceeds southward, and enters the Weald of Sussex through Tilgate Forest, and to the Balcombe tunnel.

BALCOMBE

Distance from station, 1 mile. A telegraph station. Money Order Office at Cuckfield.

To the left, on the hills, is *Wakehurst Place*, the estate of Sir A. Cockburn, St Leonard's Forest on the right. The rivers Adur, Arun, and Ouse have their source in this forest, within a circle of three or four miles in diameter.

A short distance further on the line crosses the Ouse by the viaduct of that name, one of the finest works in the kingdom, which is only excelled by the viaduct over the Dee on the Chester and Shrewsbury Hallway. It consists of thirty-seven arches, and its summit commands extensive views of the surrounding country.

As we are whirled along it, the prospect presents us with an unbounded scene of beauty, the country round being steeped in the most luxuriant verdure, and hill and dale, woodland and pasture land, succeed each other in infinite variety to the very verge of the horizon.

HAYWARD'S HEATH (Junction)

Distance from station, 1 1/4 mile. A telegraph station. Market Day – Friday, at Cuckfield. Fairs – April 23rd and Nov. 18th, on the heath; Sept. 16th and Thursday in Whit-week, at Cuckfield. Money Order Office at Cuckfield.

Hayward's Heath to Lewes and Newhaven Branch – see page 91.

HAYWARD'S HEATH TO BRIGHTON

Two miles to the right of Hayward's Heath is Cuckfield, a pleasantly situated market town, which has a handsome church in a picturesque spot The neighbourhood of Lindfield on the other side is also very beautiful.

A cutting of nearly two miles leads us to an embankment over St John's Common. Four miles farther is the station at

BURGESS HILL

A telegraph station. Money Order Office at Hurst.

The line passes through a beautiful, cultivated, and fertile country to ...

Balcombe/Wakehurst Place
The quietest station on the Brighton main line. Notable for the nineteenth-century graffiti scratched by a striking train crew into the rock on the down platform which reads, 'WFC – The Strike of the LBSCR Engine Drivers – Tuesday 26 March 1867, *top left*. Wakehurst Place is now an outstation of Kew Gardens and is home to the Millenium Seed Bank, *top right*. *(Simon Jeffs)* Between Balcombe and Copyhold Junction (where the branch from Horsted Keynes trails in from the left), the line crosses the lofty Ouse Valley Viaduct, *above*. *(John Scrace)*

Middle left: Hassocks station, which was totally rebuilt in 2013. *(Simon Jeffs)*

Bottom left: Haywards Heath was originally the railhead for Lindfield and Cuckfield. Rebuilt by Southern Railway in 1932 when the line was electrified. *(Laurel Arnison)*

HASSOCK'S GATE

A telegraph station. Money Order Office at Hurst.

From the Hassock's Gate station, a graceful piece of Gothic architecture marks the entrance to the Clayton tunnel, which is cut through blocks of chalk. These enormous chalk hills are composed of lime, in chemical combination with carbonic gas, the same which sparkles in a bottle of soda water; and if nature had not combined these substances, the first shower of rain would raise the lime to a great heat, and these stalwart cliffs would crumble into atoms.

On the left is Ditchling Beacon, 864 feet high, on the South Downs, where about a half a million of prime sheep are fed. The train thence passes Clayton and Patcham tunnels. On the right is Devil's Dyke, noted for its extensive view over the woodland in the Weald. As the train approaches the village of Preston, and the platform of the Brighton terminus, the guards collect the tickets, and the passenger has an opportunity of noting the two branch lines that diverge from Preston, one across the Preston viaduct to Lewes, and the other through a deep cutting towards Shoreham, Worthing, Chichester, and Portsmouth.

BRIGHTON

Population, 87,317. A telegraph station.

Hotels – The Bedford Hotel; Royal York; Bristol; Old Ship; Pier; the Clarence, etc.

Omnibuses to and from the station and Hove every train, and Shoreham, daily. Market days – Tuesday (corn), and Saturday. Fairs – Holy Thursday, and September 4th.

Bankers – The Brighton Union Bank; Hall, West & Co; London & County Bank.

The Brighton terminus is an elegant structure, fitted up in the most convenient manner. There is a portico in the Roman architectural style, which projects on pillars into the street, and is surmounted by an illuminated clock.

This once famous resort of royalty and fashion may now, through the literal as well as metaphorical levelling of the railroad, be fairly entitled to the appellation of the Marine Metropolis. Merchants who formerly made Dulwich or Dalston the boundaries of their suburban residences, now have got their mansions on the south coast, and still get in less time, by a less expensive conveyance, to their counting-houses in the city. Excursions are now made with greater facility, and possibly more enjoyment, to Brighton, than would have, a few years back, sufficed for the common-place pilgrimage to Hampton Court; and a constant succession of trains, conveying a host of pleasure-seekers and business men to and fro, now traverse with marvellous frequency and precision the line that has sprung, by the magical enterprise of man, from tracts of waving corn-fields and boundless breadths of pasture.

About, two miles from Brighton, Hollingbury Hill – no mean eminence of itself – stretches northward towards Lowes, and occupies a conspicuous position in the landscape. Before you is a majestic range of buildings – such as perhaps no other town in the kingdom can boast – sweeping down the sides of the cliff in every direction, and sheltering the three miles of architectural magnificence which forms the sea frontage, whilst beyond spreads the swelling sea, an object of such grandeur as in its

Above: Between Hassocks and Preston Park, the line passes through Clayton Tunnel, surmounted by its castellated northern entrance. It was the scene of a terrible accident between three trains on 25 August 1861, which led to major improvements in signalling practices *(Colin Scott-Morton)*
Below: The Preston Viaduct. *(Michael Baker)*

Brighton

... or London-by-Sea, as it is sometimes known, was the progenitor of nearly all the 'traditional' seaside towns. The ancient settlement of 'Brighthelmstone' dates from before the Domesday Book (1086), but it was the eighteenth-entury fashion for drinking and bathing in seawater, popularised by Dr Richard Russell of Lewes who sent many of his rich patrons to 'take the cure' at Brighton, that put the town on the map as a health resort. Growth was further encouraged by the patronage of the Prince Regent from 1783, who spent much of his leisure time here and constructed the Royal Pavilion. The arrival of the London & Brighton Railway in 1841 brought hordes of day-trippers from London, with the population growing from 7,000 in 1801 to 120,000 by 1901.

Top right: The commodious terminus designed by Moccata. This was substantially rebuilt to give the beautiful station we know today, middle right, with its arching roofs, decorated stanchions and pillars and LBSCR clock. *(Simon Jeffs)*

The LBSCR established its Brighton Works in 1870, shown bottom right.

29

Volk's Electric Railway

No railway enthusiast should miss a trip on Volk's Electric Railway along the seafront by the Place Pier towards Black Rock. This was Britain's first public electric railway, opened in 1883 and still going strong. *(Simon Jeffs)* Today the line runs between terminals at Aquarium, a short distance from the Palace Pier, and Black Rock near the Marina, with a depot at Paston Place which is now known as Halfway. Brighton Corporation took control of the line in 1940. It was closed during the Second World War and reopened in 1948. The Volk's Electric Railway Association was formed in 1995 to help with the promotion and operation of the line. *Left:* Postcard showing the Electric Railway being battered by the sea. *(CMcC)*

Below: Brighton's Palace Pier bathed in sunshine. *(Simon Jeffs)*

ever-changeful expanse to outvie the lavish richness with which art has fringed its cliffs and shingled shores.

As will be at once apparent on descending the street leading from the station, the town is seated on an eminence that declines gradually towards the south-east, with a sloping undulation towards the Steyne, and then again ascends to the eastward. The twang of saltness that greets the lip, and the freshening, invigorating tone of the breeze, are agreeable proofs, on your first entrance, of the bracing bleak atmosphere that characterises the climate, though in various portions of the town, more sheltered, the air will be found adapted to the exigencies of the most delicate invalid. The panoramic view that first bursts upon the eye is so striking of itself that it may be worthwhile glancing at it in detail, for the benefit of the visitor's future peregrinations.

To the left are seen two noble turfed enclosures, both thickly planted with shrubs, and laid out in the style of our metropolitan squares. The further section, intersected by a road, is the old Steyne, in the northern enclosure of which is Chantrey's bronze statue of His Majesty the fourth George, erected in 1828, at a cost of £3,000, collected among the visitors and inhabitants. This memorial crowns the square, and, as it were, points out the actual founder of the magnificence and is fretted with greater variety than taste, is – we cannot say how long it will remain – the Marine Pavilion of her Majesty, erected for George the Fourth, after a fanciful oriental model, which, despite its supposed resemblance to the Moscow Kremlin, has had no precedent before or since. Adjoining are the royal stables, the main architecture of which is a vast glazed dome, lighting a circle of about 250 feet. It will be seen that the chief streets are not only wide and handsome, but well paved and brilliantly lighted, whilst the shops are of absolute metropolitan magnificence, with goods equalling In quality, and, on the average, not much excelling in price, the wares destined for a London sale. The profusion of squares, terraces, crescents, and Steynes, with the bold beauty of the esplanade itself, produces a pleasing impression of variety, enhanced by the amphitheatre of hills that enclose the town beneath, and loom out in startling relief against the summer sky. The groups of animated nature identified at the comer of every thoroughfare, and the busy stragglers of the streets, are all of the marked watering-place description – pleasure seekers, out for the day, and eager to be ubiquitous, hurrying to and fro, through the market, to the spa, the race-course, the windmill, the beach, the shops, and the chain-pier, In as rapid succession as the most ingenious locomotion could devise. Then appear invalids, trundled out in bath chairs on to the Parade, to catch the earliest sunbeams; scores of laughing, chubby, thoughtless children, skilled manifestly in the art of ingeniously tormenting maids, tutors, governesses, and mammas; prawn-sellers and shell-fish hawkers a few, and flymen a multitude, all idly vociferating, whilst, intent upon their customary constitutional walk, the morning *habitues* of the promenade swing lustily past. Let us mingle with the throng, and obtain a closer intimacy with, the principal features of the place.

Kemp Town – the most magnificent range of private dwellings in the kingdom – is on the estate of Thomas Read Kemp, Esq., of Black Rock, at the eastern extremity of Brighton, and is fronted by an esplanade, which is a delectable spot whereon to cultivate the intellectual. On a clear day the eye may reach from Beachy Head to the

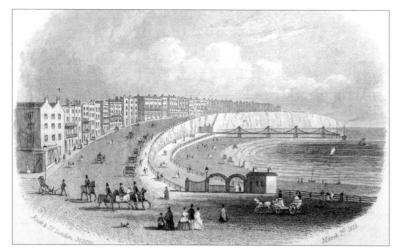

Brighton's Piers

Left: Engraving of Brighton's Marine Parade and Chain Pier. Designed by Captain Samuel Brown and built in 1823, it was officially called the Royal Suspension Pier and consisted of an esplanade with an entrance toll booth and various attractions including a camera obscura.

Many of Brighton's major attractions were built during the mid to late Victorian era; the Grand Hotel (1864), the West Pier (1866) and the Palace Pier (1899), shown left. *(CMcC)*

Rough Sea. Winter Gardens Palace Pier Brighton   R.S. 26

Below left: Little remains of the West Pier. It was closed in 1975 and despite various plans to restore it the structure has progressively deteriorated after two fires and several storms. *(Tony Hisgett)*

In 2000, Brighton was granted city status by Queen Elizabeth II as part of the millennium celebrations.

Isle of Wight, catching between the points many a bold outline of cliff and crag. The cliff here is 150 feet high, and the tunnel under the road, cut through the rock from the centre of the crescent lawn, is a very ingenious mode of shortening the distance to the lower esplanade. From Kemp Town a brisk walk over odoriferous downs brings us to Rottingdean, a village rather peculiar than either pretty or picturesque. It is famous chiefly for its wells, which are empty at high water, and full to overflowing at ebb tide. There is, however, an excellent inn for the accommodation of company, unexceptionable in the quality of its fare.

Returning past the old Steyne, we arrive opposite Mahomed's baths; in the busiest part of Brighton. Here we find fishermen mending their nets, boats laid up for repair, the fish-market and vendors engaged in every characteristic employment to be met with in a maritime town. Here also are pleasure-boats and sailing-vessels to be hired, where, if a party club together, a few hours' sail may be compassed for a dozen shillings. From hero the Market Hall is but a short distance; it stands on the site of the old Town Hall, and was built in 1830. It answers every purpose in being spacious, unconfined, and well supplied daily with fresh and fine comestibles. The new Town Hall – a vast pile of building, with three double porticoes – cost £30,000, and has a handsome assembly-room on the upper story, rendered available for divers purposes of provincial legislation and amusement.

A few, very few, years back, the battery was on the western verge of the town, and beyond it the several houses seemed to be fairly in the country. A quiet hotel or two, and a bathing establishment, reminded us that we were still in Brighton, and a solitary villa, belonging to the Countess St Antonio – a kind of Italianized cottage, with two wings, then the scene of many a gay rout notwithstanding its humility – just kept the fashion of the place in mind as, many a time and oft, we lingered on the rough and barren road to Shoreham, strewn with the flowers of hoar antiquity.

The line of extension has now become almost interminable, and most conspicuous in the elongation of the western esplanade is Brunswick-terrace, built from the designs of Mr Busby, a son of Mr Busby, of musical memory. The terrace consists of forty-two splendid houses, and has a very majestic aspect. Between the two great divisions of the frontal line lies Brunswick-square, open to the sea towards the south, and the whole is fronted by an artificial esplanade, which extends a mile in length. Along this delightful walk the votaries of fashion are wont to exercise their 'recreant limbs', and recruit their wasted energies with the invigorating sea-breeze.

Above: This charming postcard shows the Floral Hall in Brighton, and was posted by a visitor to the Spring Races in 1907. 'The weather at Whitsun has not been so cold for the last forty years,' writes the sender. *(CMcC)*

Below: 1826 view showing the Banqueting Room of the Royal Pavilion, Brighton. *(LoC)*

The chain-pier, which has been for years entitled to the first consideration of the Brighton visitor is well worthy of being still considered its greatest lion.

Hazlitt has said, 'there is something in being near the sea like the confines of eternity. It is a new element, a pure abstraction.' The mind loves to hover on that which is endless and ever the same, and the wide expanse which is here visible gratifies his feeling to the uttermost. The approaches to the pier are handsome and spacious, and the reading-room at the north end, with its camera above, is a delightful lounge for the promenader, who, having inhaled health by instalments of breathing, may therein plunge into the world of fiction, and enjoy a perusal of the last new novel with the zest of a marine atmosphere.

Churches, chapels, and meeting-houses, of all ages and for all denominations, are plentifully strewn over the town. The most modern is the handsome church of St Peter's, erected about twenty years ago, in the best pointed style, by Sir C. Barry, the well-known architect of the new Houses of Parliament. But the oldest, and perhaps the most interesting, is the ancient parish church of St Nicholas, standing on the summit of a hill at the north-west extremity of the town. It is an excellent sea and land-mark, and is said to be as old as the reign of Henry VII. From this pleasant locality the esplanade and parade are seen to much advantage. Gay loiterers of pleasure, and donkey parties, regiments of schools, and old bathing women, literary loungers, who read out of doors, and stumble against lamp-posts in interesting passages – these, and a host of other peripatetic humanities, make the beach populous between Hove and Kemp Town.

With regard to inns, taverns, hotels, lodging and boarding-houses, nowhere are they more numerous than here, their excellence of accommodation of course varying with price. Bathing establishments, too, are almost as numerous, whilst, for amusements, there is no provincial town in the kingdom that can offer such a variety of assembly and concert-rooms, libraries, bazaars, and other expedients for slaughtering our common enemy – Time. In the New-road is the theatre – one of the prettiest out of London – and close adjoining is the Post-office, concerning which, in these economical days of epistolary communication, it may be as well to know the precise hours of dispatch and delivery.

The race-course is about a mile and a half northward of the town, on the summit of one of the loftiest and most commanding downs in the neighbourhood. The races generally take place early in August.

As the Brighton excursionist will go to the Devil's Dyke, as a matter of course, we do not stay to tell him how he shall behold therefrom the Isle of Wight, spread beneath him like a map, or Beechy Head, looming like a snow-peak to the east, and the Downs far away, mingling with the horizon. But be it gently whispered, that on the margin of this demoniacal defile there standeth a small hostel, the glories of whose bread and cheese and ale have been sung by many an aristocratic voice. Everybody that ever was there assures you that for baking and brewing it stands unrivalled, although we shrewdly suspect that the preparatory course of Southdown oxygen hath a wonderful agency in eliciting this appreciation of a fare so humble.

Brighton and Lewes Branch – see page 51.

LONDON BRIGHTON & SOUTH COAST RAILWAY.

COAST LINE RAIL MOTOR SERVICES

ALL THE YEAR ROUND.

BETWEEN

St. LEONARDS AND EASTBOURNE | **BRIGHTON AND WORTHING** | **CHICHESTER AND PORTSMOUTH**

COPYRIGHT 8597   WATERLOW & SONS LTD LITH LONDON WALL LONDON   WILLIAM FORBES, *General Manager.*

The Coastal Lines

BRIGHTON–CHICHESTER ON THE PORTSMOUTH LINE

On leaving the [Brighton] terminus the line turns off abruptly towards the east, and passing through the New England tunnel, cut in the chalk cliff beneath Henfield Road, reaches the station at

HOVE

Telegraph station at Brighton, 1 mile.

This village is now a suburb, or continuation of Brighton, The old church of Hove is a fine edifice, and there is a new cross-shaped one, with a tall spire. There are fine walks here over the Downs, The summit of a high cliff in the neighbourhood, called the Devil's Dyke, is much visited for the fine views it affords of the surrounding country.

Portslade and Southwick stations.

KINGSTON-ON-SEA

A telegraph station. Hotel – Kingston Inn. Money Order Office at Shoreham.

This village is situated on the right of the line; it has a harbour and wharf, and is said to be prosperous and thriving. The line proceeds along the shore, presenting no feature worth remarking, and reaches ...

Above: Hove railway station opened in May 1840 on the line from Shoreham-by-Sea to Brighton – before the main line from London to the harbour at Shoreham. The current station, opened in 1865 was originally named Cliftonville, then West Brighton, before being renamed Hove and West Brighton in 1894 and finally Hove in 1895! *(Simon Jeffs)*

Shoreham

The town and port of Shoreham-by-Sea is actually known as New Shoreham and was established by the Normans in the eleventh century. St Mary de Haura Church (St Mary of the Haven) was built after 1103 and the new town around it laid out on a grid pattern that survives in the town centre to this day. Old Shoreham dates back to pre-Roman and St Nicolas' Church, inland by the River Adur, is partly Anglo-Saxon, *top left*. The Grade II* Shoreham Tollbridge crosses the River Adur in the west of the town and was the last toll bridge in use in Sussex. Originally opened in 1782, it was part of the A27 road until closed to traffic in 1968. Following restoration, the bridge reopened for pedestrians on 23 October 2008. Shoreham is unique in having road, rail and air links. The original terminus built by the London & Brighton Railway opened on 11 May 1840, *left*. Shoreham Airport, *below*, is to the west of the town and next to the railway where there was once a station. It is the UK's oldest licensed airport and has a superb 1936 Art Deco terminal building. *(Simon Jeffs)*

NEW SHOREHAM

A telegraph station. Hotels – Surrey Arms, Buckingham Arms, and Swiss Cottage.

Market Day – Every alternate Monday (corn). Fair – July 25th.

Old Shoreham, on the right of the line, has a fine old Saxon church, which has been recently restored, and is much admired as a beautiful specimen of Saxon architecture.

New Shoreham is a borough town and a port, situated at the mouth of the River Adur, over which there is a suspension bridge. The harbour is about a mile to the eastward of the town.

The Swiss Gardens, a kind of Vauxhall, are beautiful. The grounds are admirably laid out, and a constant succession of amusements provided in exchange for the shilling that entitles you to the admission. The cottage is called the 'Swiss Cottage' – not that the peasants are so lodged in Switzerland, but that in novels and noblemen's parks structures of one story high are thus denominated. The material must have cost less than the workmanship, for the doors, windows, and less substantial parts of the fabric are composed of little pieces of stick with the hark on – not expensive by any means, but so picturesque, as a young lady will be sure to remark within your hearing. Inside this Helvetian habitation there is a *salon a manger*, on a great scale, besides several little saloons for refreshment and flirtation, being, in fact, refectories for two inside – the most compact and comfortable places you can imagine. Added to this, there is a little theatre, a concert, music, swings, and oracles of divination, for all who choose to consult the mystic temple of the Sybil. Of the whole place it may be said, with justice, that there is not in England another so well designed, or preserved in such excellent order.

Few districts in England exhibit more interesting relics of the early history of the island than this part of Sussex. Shoreham was certainly a place of importance previous to the Conquest. Subsequently its geographical position must have added still more to its consequence. From the Downs to Portsmouth the coast is, even in our day, most difficult of access – ten centuries ago it was without a landing-place for vessels of burden, or for craft of any sort, with strong winds from three points of the compass, except Newhaven and Shoreham. As easterly winds are – happily for folks of rheumatic tendency – more rare than any others for nine months in the year, these two places probably monopolised all the intercourse between Great Britain and her French territories. For this reason splendid and unique specimens of Norman architecture abound in Sussex. Of these, not one of the least remarkable is the parish church of New Shoreham. It was originally formed as a crucifix, and covered a great deal of ground. The embellishments are still of rare richness and variety, and are full of interest as marks of the state of the arts in those remote days.

Littlehampton and Arundel

Arundel and Littlehampton station opened in 1850 on the main line which closed when the branch to the town opened in August 1863. A port town, the arrival of the railway made it a holiday destination and a cross-channel ferry to Honfleur in France was introduced. It remains a commercial port and major centre for leisure craft, with a thriving marina. The station was totally rebuilt in 1987 and in 2013 celebrated its 150th anniversary, *left. (Simon Jeffs)*

Left: Arundel was connected to the railway system when the Mid-Sussex line was extended south from Pulborough to Ford junction, opening two weeks before the branch to Littlehampton in 1863. The station is outside of the town, making it less than ideal for tourists, but sees a good number of commuters. *(Stuart Hicks)* Arundel can become very crowded with visitors thronging to the castle, *below*, and Wildfowl and Wetlands Trust. *(Gregg M. Erickson)*

LANCING STATION

Is close to the pretty 'sea-side' village of that name, known as Lancing-by-Sea, which is in some repute as a quiet, retired bathing-place, but it is excessively dull and *ennuyant*.

Telegraph station at Worthing, 2 ½ miles. Hotels – The Farmer's, and Sussex Pad.

A few miles beyond this we reach the more important station and town of

WORTHING

Population, 5,805. A telegraph station. Hotels – Sea House and Steyne.
Omnibuses to and from the station and Storrington.
Market Days – Wednesday (corn), and Saturday. Fair – July 20th.

This market town has lately become very fashionable as a watering-place. Its rise from an insignificant hamlet to its present rank has been rapid almost beyond precedent, even in the annals of this coast. It is said to owe this distinction to the superior mildness of its temperature, arising from the shelter afforded by the Downs, which, at the distance of scarcely a mile, environ it, and exclude the chilling blasts of the northern and eastern winds, rendering bathing practicable even in the depth of winter. The climate is perhaps somewhat relaxing. The sands, extending nearly ten miles in length, are level, hard, and compact, and afford a beautiful ride or walk. Like Brighton, the town follows the line of the sea, the esplanade extending for three-quarters of a mile along the shore. Towards the close of a summer or autumnal evening no more delightful promenade can be imagined than this beach, as it echoes to the hollow murmuring of the waves, rippled with the sea breeze, whilst afar off can be seen the gas-lights of the town of Brighton, forming a continuous chain of beads of light.
The line proceeds three miles further on, and reaches the station at

GORING

Telegraph station at Worthing, 2 ½ miles. Money Order Office at Worthing.

After which an additional four miles bring us to the station at ...

Throughout the centuries this part of the coast has been at the front line facing hostile forces coming from the Continent. In the Second World War it saw more than its share of the Luftwaffe's aircraft.

Above: A lone sentry stands guard over the wreck of a Junkers Ju 88 bomber, which has come down on the shoreline in the Littlehampton area. Part of his job was to keep souvenir hunters away until the wreck could be salvaged.

Left: A member of the RAF is brought ashore after a ditching in the Channel. *(CMcC)*

ANGMERING

Telegraph station at Arundel, 2 1/4 miles. Money Order Office at Arundel.

The line passes through a fine and highly cultivated country, and reaches the station at

LITTLEHAMPTON

A short distance from a small hamlet on the coast, which has some admirers as a retired watering place.

Telegraph station at Arundel, 8 miles. Hotels – Norfolk, George, and New.
Mails – Two arrivals and departures, daily, between London and Littlehampton.
Money Order Office.

ARUNDEL

A telegraph station. Distance from station, 2 miles.
Hotel – Norfolk. Omnibuses to and from Storrington thrice weekly.
Market Days – Monday and Saturday. Fairs – May 14th, August 21st, Sept. 25th, and Dec. 17th. Money Order Office. Bankers – London & County Bank; Henty & Co.

Arundel is situated on the declivity of a steep hill, which commands a fine prospect. At the foot of this eminence runs the river Arun, over which is built a handsome stone bridge. From the Worthing Road the appearance of the town, with its stately castle, extensive park, and winding river, is singularly beautiful. On the north-east part of the town stands the Castle, which has the remarkable privilege of: entitling its owner to the dignity of an earl without creation. It is in the possession of the Howard family. The late Duke of Norfolk restored it to its former magnificence, and it is now one of the most elegant Gothic residences in England. The situation of the castle is one of great beauty. It stands on an eminence, embosomed in a luxuriant grove, and commands a fine and extensive view of the surrounding country, the sea, and the Isle of Wight.

FORD

A telegraph station. Money Order Office at Arundel.

YAPTON

Telegraph station at Arundel, 3 miles. Distance from the station, 1 mile.
Money Order Office at Arundel.

The line passes on a level, with the open sea on one side and the South Downs on the other, and reaches the station at ...

Bugger Bognor

In a document of AD 680, Bognor is referred to as Bucgan ora meaning Bucge's (a female Anglo-Saxon name) shore, or landing place. Now, its fame rests on Butlins, birdmen and 'Bugger Bognor!' Tourism gradually developed during the nineteenth-century, with King George V convalescing in the area during 1929. As a result, the King was asked to bestow the suffix 'Regis' ('of the King') on Bognor. When the petition was delivered to the King, he supposedly replied, 'Oh, bugger Bognor!'

Sir Billy Butlin opened one of his holiday camps in Bognor in 1960. The camp later became known as Southcoast World until 1998 and is now known as Butlins Bognor Regis. The International Bognor Birdman is an annual competition for human-powered 'flying' machines who launch themselves from the end of Bognor's pier, *below*. The station was originally opened in June 1864, at the end of a branch line from Barnham, *top left*. The current station dates from 1902 after the previous facility burnt down in 1899. *(Simon Jeffs)*

WOODGATE

A telegraph station. Distance from station, 3/4 mile. Hotels – Claremont, Norfolk.

Mails – One arrival and departure, daily, between London and Woodgate.

Money Order Office at Arundel.

The station of Woodgate communicates with Rognor, a pleasant bathing place, towards the south.

BOGNOR

Population, 2,523. Telegraph station at Woodgate, 1 1/2 mile.

Hotels – York and Norfolk. Money Order Office.

Bognor is a pleasant bathing place, with good beach, crescent, etc., and much frequented, the air being very pure, and the situation delightful. It was made a market town in 1822, and owes its rise to Sir Richard Hotham, in 1785.

DRAYTON

Telegraph station at Chichester, 2 miles. Distance from station, 1/2 mile.

Money Order Office at Chichester.

CHICHESTER

Population, 8,059. A telegraph station. Hotel – Dolphin.

Coaches to and from Godalming, daily; Petworth, and Midhurst, thrice weekly.

Market Days – Wednesdays and Saturdays. Fairs – St George's Day, Whit Monday, St James's Day, Michaelmas Day, and ten days after. Money Order Office.

Bankers – London and County Bank; Cooper & Co.

Like Chester, Chichester is an old town on the square Roman plan, but the marks of antiquity are less decided; The Romans called it *Regni*, but Cista, the king of the south Saxons christened it *Cisaceaster*, from which the modern name is corrupted. It is a clean neatly built cathedral city and parliamentary borough (returns two members), in *Sussex*, on the South Coast Railway, 16 miles from Portsmouth. Four principal streets within the site of the ancient walls intersect at the middle, where stands Bishop Story's decorated English *Market Cross*. This prelate also founded the *Grammar School*, 1497, in which Archbishop Juxom, the learned Selden, and Collins and Hardis, the poets, were educated. The *Guildhall* was once the chapel to a friary. The last of the four gates was removed when the gaol was built, 1783. There are eight churches, some of which suffered in the civil war, two being actually dismantled, by the royalists, 1642, to strengthen the walls.

The **Cathedral** is a cross building of the 12th century, 314 feet long, or 377 feet with the Lady chapel, and 133 feet through the transept. Norman and early English work prevails in the nave and the north transept. The Lady chapel, over the Richmond vault, was built about 1300, and contains the library of old books. Several new stained windows have

Chichester

Above: Chichester railway station opened in 1847, but the current facility is a 1960s-built structure of some architectural merit. The station booking hall, *top right*, is exceptionally busy, particularly with schoolchildren and tourists. *(Simon Jeffs)*

The city and surrounding area has an ancient history, founded by the Romans, as evidenced by the nearby Fishbourne Roman Palace.The city centre stands on the foundations of the Romano-British city of Noviomagus Reginorum. The Roman road of Stane Street, connecting the city with London, started at the east gate, while the Chichester to Silchester road started from the north gate. The plan of the city is inherited from the Romans: the North, South, East and West shopping streets radiate from the central market cross, shown left, dating from medieval times. The city is the administrative and legal centre for West Sussex, a major commercial centre and home to a small university, several art galleries, museums and the renowned Chichester Festival Theatre. *(Simon Jeffs)*

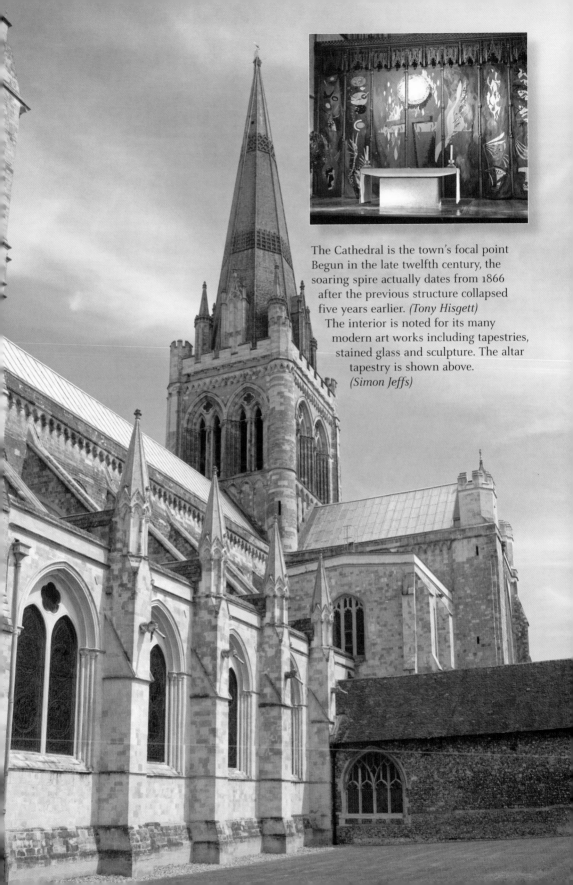

The Cathedral is the town's focal point Begun in the late twelfth century, the soaring spire actually dates from 1866 after the previous structure collapsed five years earlier. *(Tony Hisgett)* The interior is noted for its many modern art works including tapestries, stained glass and sculpture. The altar tapestry is shown above. *(Simon Jeffs)*

Goodwood

Five miles north from Chichester lies Goodwood,
with its racecourse and Goodwood House (the seat of
the Duke of Richmond), famous for its annual motor
racing event, the Festival of Speed, which was founded
in 1993 to bring motor racing back to the Goodwood
estate. Since 1997 a major feature has been the central
displays erected on the front lawns. Each successive
year these temporary monuments, all designed by
Gerry Judah, have astounded visitors and defied
gravity. This image featuring Porsches is from the
2013 event. *(Peter Castleton)*
Inset: Lotus 21 at Goodwood in 2012. *(Darren)*

been added lately. In the north aisle is Flaxman's monument to Collins (who was born here 1720) reading the best of books, as Johnson describes him in his last days. Another monument to *Huskisson* the statesman. Bernardi's paintings in the style of Holbein, and a series of so-called portraits of kings and bishops since the Conquest may be noticed. In the cloisters called 'Paradise', 200 feet long, is the monument of *Chillingworth* the great 'propugnator invictissimus' (i.e., invincible *bruiser* of the Protestants) who died here, 1643. He was a man of little stature, but a great controversialist, so that Anthony a Wood said, 'If the great Turk or the devil could be converted, he was able to do it.' At the north-west corner is the bell tower, 120 feet high, standing by itself. The fine eight-sided spire is 300 feet high. At the Bishop's *Palace* is a chapel partly as old as Henry III, and an old timber-roofed hall and kitchen. It was first built by Bishop Sherborne about 1530. Selsey (8 miles) near Selsey Bill, in the English Channel, was the seat of the bishopric, till it was moved to Chichester by the Normans, 1075. There is an old church. The sea now covers the site of some monastic buildings.

Goodwood (three miles), seat of the Duke of Richmond, stands in a large park under the South Downs. Hero the July races are held, and which arc always attended by the *haut ton* and the leading members of the Turf. It is about six miles round, and well wooded, and contains two cork trees, and about 1,000 cedars, planted 1762. From the grotto on Cairney seat (built out of a ruined church), is a fine view of the coast, Isle of Wight, the Downs, etc. The house was built by Sir W. Chambers, and enlarged by Wyattville, with centre and wings. It is 378 feet long, the wings falling back at angles of 45 feet. Stone and flint are used. In the hall is a standard and other trophies from Waterloo (which the late Duke attended as an amateur). The drawing room is 58 feet long. One portrait is that of a beautiful Duchess of Richmond of Charles II's time – the original, it is said, of Britannia on the copper coinage. Large stables and dog kennels with a tennis-court, are behind.

[Beyond Chichester the line passes across the border into Hampshire to continue westwards to Havant and Portsmouth.]

Right: The LBSCR line reached Havant from Chichester in 1847. On 28 December 1858, the first LSWR train from Waterloo was supposed to arrive, but a serious altercation broke out between the two companies resulting in points being lifted, engines seized and the possibility of violence until the LSWR train returned to Guildford. All is quiet now, and the current station is an SR rebuild from the electrification of 1937/8.
(Simon Jeffs)

Above left: Berwick station. *(Lester Hayes)* This is the railhead for the Cuckmere Valley and a bus connects with trains on Sundays visiting attractions in the locality, such as Drusilla's Zoo, Michelham Priory and the beautiful village of Alfriston, *above right.* Beachy Head, to the south-west of Eastbourne, is shown below. *(Simon Jeffs)*

Left: Polegate, a railhead for the north of Eastbourne and Willingdon. The first station opened in 1846 on the LBSCR line from Brighton to Hastings. A second station was built a little to the east in 1881, when the junction for the branch line from Polegate to Hailsham was rerouted and extended to Eridge. This line closed in 1968, but part of it forms the 'Cuckoo Trail' walk. In 1986, this station was closed and replaced by the present facility, on the site of the first. The platform faces of the 1881 station remain. *(Simon Jeffs)*

EASTWARDS FROM BRIGHTON

Brighton and Lewes branch

The Preston viaduct of this short line is a magnificent structure, consisting of an elliptic arch 50 feet span, and 73 feet high, flanked on one side by eighteen, and on the other by nine semi-circular arches, 30 feet span; the former are built on a curve of three-quarters of a mile radius, and the latter on a 10 chain radius. The length of the viaduct is 400 yards, and ten millions of bricks were used in the construction. In consequence of its being on the curve, one side is above 40 feet longer than the other; all the arcades radiate towards the centre of the curve, and the piers are one foot eight inches thicker at one end than the other, in order to render the openings parallel. The viaduct is universally admired for its beautiful proportions. The view from its summit is exceedingly fine. On the elevated ground to the right is the extensive terminus of the Brighton Railway, and in front lies the town of Brighton and its fine expanse of sea.

After crossing the above viaduct, the line passes through a short tunnel (sixty yards) beneath the Ditchling Road, and the deep chalk cuttings on either side. Just beyond the cutting a bridge crosses the road, forming the northern boundary of the parish of Brighton. After passing through another cutting of considerable length and depth, the line extends along the side of the hill at the back of the Cavalry Barracks, and consists of embankment and cutting combined. Another cutting brings us to Moulscombe, a neat villa, the grounds of which are bisected by the railway, and again connected by a bridge. A deep cutting leads us to Hodshrove, where the Lewes turnpike road is crossed by a skew-bridge of three arches, which are of noble proportions and of massive strength. From this point, the line which had hitherto run on the western side of the Lewes road, lies entirely on the eastern side. A high embankment and deep cutting follow; and we then pass another long one, skirting the front of the Earl of Chichester's Bark at Stammer. This is the most beautiful domain on the line; the estate comprehends the whole parish and village of Stammer, including the church. The park occupies a valley formed by one of those bold ranges of hills which adorn the coasts of this county; and its undulating surface, varied by thick masses of foliage, forms a rich contrast to the open downs by which it is environed. The Stammer elevation brings us to the foot of

FALMER

Telegraph station at Lewes, 4 3/4 miles. Hotel – Swan.
Money Order Office at Lewes and Brighton.

A deep cutting commences here, which is succeeded by a tunnel, followed by another deep cutting; then a shorter one, and we obtain a sight of Lewes, St Anne's Church and the Castle being the most prominent objects. Nothing remarkable occurs after this till we reach the foot of Water Shoot Hill, where the railway crosses the Winterbourne, and taking a course to the right by a short tunnel enters Southover, passing under the road which leads from Lewes to Newhaven. It then crosses the priory grounds, and thus arrives at the station at **Lewes**, which is in High Street, at the foot of School Hill.

Eastbourne

Situated immediately east of Beachy Head, this sheltered position contributes to Eastbourne's title of sunniest place in Great Britain. In Bradshaw's day the town was rapidly gaining favour as a fashionable resort, largely thanks to the town's prominent landowner, the Duke of Devonshire, who was responsible for the Victorian architecture. The seafront consists almost entirely of Victorian hotels which, along with its pier, gardens, bandstand and the absence of shops and pubs has preserved the look of the front in a timeless manner. Although sometimes unfairly criticised as being 'God's waiting room', it actually has a major student, commuting and family demographic and attracts many tourists, particularly for the annual 'Airbourne' free, international airshow and the Devonshire Park Lawn Tennis tournament. The line to Eastbourne from Polegate was opened by the LBSCR in 14 May 1849. *Top:* The current station is the third, designed by F. D. Brick in 1886, with a vaulted canopy and lantern roof similar to Lewes. It has some interesting little touches, including a fine gargoyle. *(Simon Jeffs)*

Lewes – see Haywards Heath to Lewes Branch Line on page 91.

FROM LEWES TO HAILSHAM, EASTBOURNE, & HASTINGS

The line from Lewes turns eastward, round the foot of Mount Cabnm, and after passing through a valley in the South Downs, reaches the station at

GLYNDE

> Distance from station, ½ mile. Telegraph station at Lewes, 3 miles.
> Money Order Office at Lewes.

The station is near the village of Glyndebourne, in the vicinity of which is *Glynde Place*, the seat of Sir J. Langham, and *Firle Place*, the property of Viscount Gage. The South Downs, at Firle Beacon, rise to the height of 820 feet.

The line then passes the villages of Selmeston and Alceston to the station at

BERWICK

> A little to the north of the village of the same name. Telegraph station at Polegate, 4 miles. Hotels – Fuller's Arms. Money Order office at Eastbourne.

Four miles beyond, the line reaches the station at

POLEGATE (Willingdon)

> Distance from station, 1 mile. A telegraph station.
> Money Order Office at Eastbourne.

Short lines branch off here in opposite directions to Hailsham and Eastbourne.

HAILSHAM (Branch)

> A telegraph station. Hotels – Turmunus, George, and Crown.
> Market Day – Wednesday (cattle). Fairs – April 6th and June 3rd. Money Order Office at Hailsham.

Hailsham, three miles from the junction, is a quiet little market town, situated on a gentle declivity. It has the remains of a priory, and the pinnacled church of Edward III's time is rather handsome.

EASTBOURNE (Branch)

> Distance from station, 1 mile. A telegraph station. Hotel – Lamb.
> Market Day – Saturday. Fairs – March 12th and October 10th.
> Money Order Office at Eastbourne.

Eastbourne has, within a very few years, become fashionable as a watering-place.

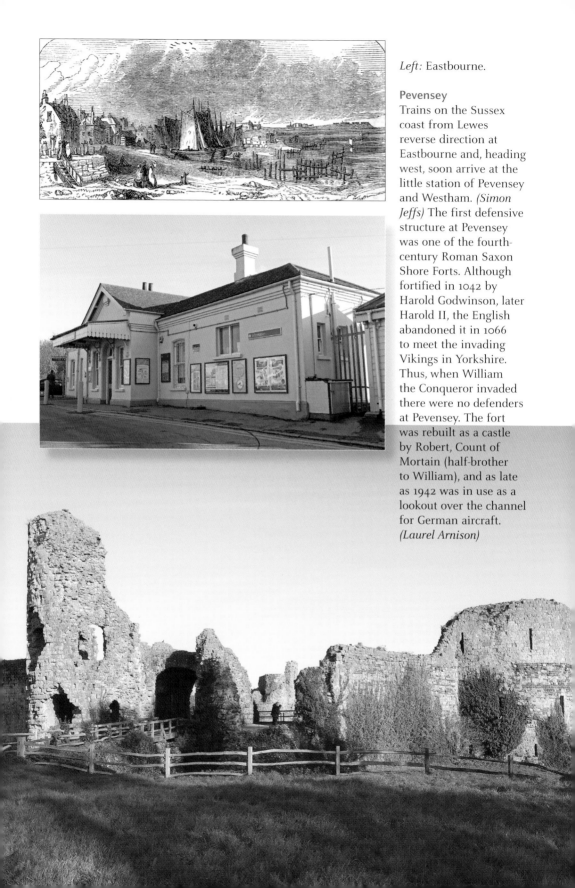

Left: Eastbourne.

Pevensey
Trains on the Sussex coast from Lewes reverse direction at Eastbourne and, heading west, soon arrive at the little station of Pevensey and Westham. *(Simon Jeffs)* The first defensive structure at Pevensey was one of the fourth-century Roman Saxon Shore Forts. Although fortified in 1042 by Harold Godwinson, later Harold II, the English abandoned it in 1066 to meet the invading Vikings in Yorkshire. Thus, when William the Conqueror invaded there were no defenders at Pevensey. The fort was rebuilt as a castle by Robert, Count of Mortain (half-brother to William), and as late as 1942 was in use as a lookout over the channel for German aircraft. *(Laurel Arnison)*

The bathing is very good, and a number of machines are employed. It has also the advantage of mineral springs, the waters of which are said to resemble those of Clifton. A theatre, a ballroom, a library, and reading-rooms are the principal attractions of the town, and there are good walks and rides. It lies about three miles west of Beachy Head, is much recommended for its bracing air, and offers the somewhat rare attrac¬tions of the beauty of country scenery and stately trees, almost dose to the sea. Eastbourne town lies about a mile and a half from the beach or sea-houses, the actual watering place. The sea-houses comprise hotels, lodging houses, baths, etc. Beachy Head on the right is a favourite excursion point. To the left is the esplanade, and further inward the large circular fort of redoubts; and in the distance several Martello towers. Eastbourne has one of the finest chruches in the country – Norman and early English.

Hastings Branch Line continued

Immediately on leaving Polegate, eastward, commences the Pevensey level, the scene of the Norman Conquest; and the coast from hence to Hastings is rich in association with this grand chapter of our civilisation.

PEVENSEY

Near the town of that name.

 Telegraph station at Polegate, 3 1/2 miles. Hotel – Royal Oak.

 Market Day – Thursday (Southdown Sheep). Fairs – July 5th and Sept. 15th.

Though formerly a place of so much importance as to give name to the hundred, it has now dwindled to an inconsiderable village; and the sea, which formerly laved the castle wails, has now receded to a distance of two miles. A number of Martello towers, erected at the time of the last war [Napoleonic] – we hope the phrase will be just as applicable for a hundred generations yet to come – remain as memorials of the means resorted to for the defence of the coast. The history of Pevenscy might be easily expanded by a skilful topographist into a volume, but a brief enumeration of the leading features will suffice to acquaint the visitor with its bygone glories. It first appears in our chronicles in A.D. 792, when honourable mention is made of it as having been generously given by Bervald, a general of Offa, to the Abbey of St Denis at Paris. In the reign of Edward the Confessor it was dignified by twenty-four burgesses, and was ravaged by Earl Godwin, falling shortly after the reign of Henry III into hopeless decay. The castle was attacked by Simon de Montfort in 1205, and, in 1339, by the partisans of Richard II, when it was bravely defended by the Lady Jane Pelham. The outer walls of the castle enclose an area of seven acres, and are about twenty feet in height. Within is a smaller fortification, moated on the north and west, and of a quadrangular form, with round towers. The entrance was formerly by a drawbridge. The eastern wall of both is the same, and stands upon a shelving eminence. The circumference of the inner wall is about 25 rods, and of the outer walls 259. When entire it must have been of great strength. Antiquaries differ about its first builders, but if not of Roman origin it is at any rate constructed of Roman materials, and, though the adjective savours somewhat of a pun, it may be added that its

Bexhill-on-Sea

Over the Pevensey Levels to Bexhill, and arriving at the station, one is immediately struck by its huge size. Prior to the 1880s, the area was served by a small station, shown left, close to the village grouped around an ancient church and manor. Following the leads of Brighton and Eastbourne, the 7th Earl De La Warr decided to transform the village into an exclusive seaside resort, which he named Bexhill-on-Sea. He was instrumental in building a sea wall south of the village, and the road above it was then named De La Warr Parade. Large houses were built inland from there, and the new town began. In 1890, the luxurious Sackville Hotel was built and the current station, dating from 1891, was ready to receive the crowds who flocked to its attractions. Photographed in 2014, it is shown left. *(Simon Jeffs)*. A second line, this time built by the SER, was a branch from Crowhurst to a terminus at Bexhill West. The line opened in 1902 but closed by 1964.

Below: The seafront is notable for the Grade I listed De La Warr Pavilion, a classic of modernist architecture erected in 1936. *(CMcC)*

present aspect is decidedly romantic. The church is but an ordinary looking structure, with a square tower at the west end. It is dedicated to St Nicholas. The rich pastures of Pevensey level afford fine grazing for cattle, and have contributed much to the profit and renown of the graziers surrounding.

The Castle of Hurstmonceaux, on an eminence five miles distant, at the end of a long valley, looks a noble and imposing structure, and, although a ruin, is in very good preservation.

The railway proceeds along the coast to the station at

BEXHILL

The village of which name is situated on a rising ground not far from the sea. It is a quiet, retired place, having some good iron springs, and is situated in a beautiful country.

Telegraph station at St Leonards, 3 miles.

Hotel – Bell. Fairs – June 28th, and 1st Monday in July.

Many persons prefer the retirement of Bexhill, with its fine bracing air, to the excitement and bustle of the neighbouring towns.

ST LEONARDS

A telegraph station. Hotel – Royal Victoria; Royal Saxon. Markets – Daily.

St Leonards – recognised 'west-end' of Hastings, with which is now connected, a fine noble archway marking the boundary of the two townships, was planned and executed by the well-known architect, Mr Decimus Burton, who only commenced his bold project in 1828. Hotels of eastern magnificence, public gardens, looking like realisations of the Arabian Nights' descriptions, libraries where the most fascinating novel gains an additional charm from the luxurious sea-fronting ottomans, on which their perusal may be indulged, together with an esplanade peerless in its promenading conveniences – these are but a few of the manifold attractions which St Leonards holds forth to tempt the errant visitor into becoming a stationary resident.

On the hill, by the railway station, as you approach Bulverhithe, may be seen the ruins of the Conqueror's Chapel, supposed to mark the spot where he landed. Recent antiquaries have laboured to prove that it must have been nearer Pevensey.

Hastings

Until the development of tourism, fishing was Hastings' major industry. The fishing fleet, based at the Stade, remains Europe's largest beach-launched fishing fleet and has been based on the same beach for at least 400, possibly 600, years. This postcard of the fishing boats, *top left*, dates from around 1900. *(CMcC)* The SER line from Battle reached the town in 1852 and became an exceedingly busy destination. A new, modern structure has recently been provided, with a very convenient bus interchange, shown in 2014, *above right*. *(Simon Jeffs)*

Below: The Stade/Rock-a-Noor area also houses a fishing museum, backed by the traditional black net houses, a smugglers museum, aquarium and the Jerwood Gallery of modern art. The Fishing Museum and East Hill funicular, photographed in 2014. *(Simon Jeffs)*

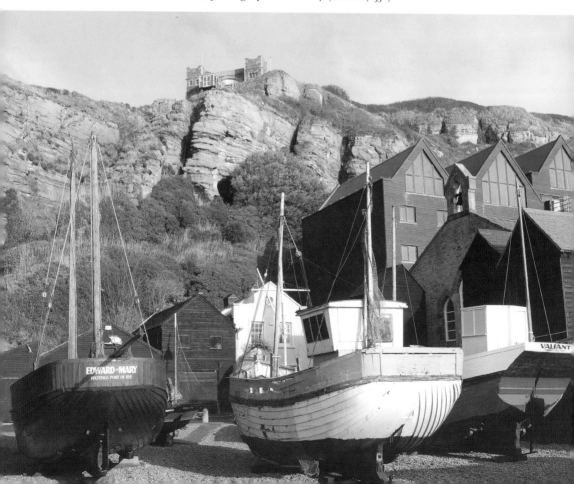

HASTINGS

Population, 22,910. A telegraph station. Hotels – The Marine, on the Parade; Albion; Castle. Omnibuses to and from the station to meet every train. Post Horses, Flys, etc., at the hotels and station, to meet every train. Market Days – Saturdays (corn); daily (poultry). Fairs – Whit Tuesday, July 26 and 29, and November 27.

The recognised salubrity and mildness of the air, together with the openness of the coast and the smoothness of the beach, have long made Hastings a favourite and a recommended resort. The shore is not abrupt, and the water almost always limpid, and of that beautiful sea-green hue so inviting to bathers. The constant surging of the waves, first breaking against the reefs, and next dashing over the sloping shingle, is not unwelcome music at midnight to the ears of all who sleep in the vicinity of the shore. Dr James Clark states, that in winter Hastings is most desirable as a place of residence during January and February.

During the spring also it has the advantage of being more effectually sheltered from north and north-east winds than any other place frequented by invalids on the coast of Sussex. It is also comparatively little subject to fogs in the spring, and the fall of rain may be said at that time to be less than on other portions of the coast. As might be expected from the low and sheltered situation of Hastings, it will be found a favourable residence generally to invalids suffering under diseases of the chest. Delicate persons, who desire to avoid exposure to the north-east winds, may pass the cold season here with all vantage. Owing to the close manner in which this place is hemmed in on the sea by steep and high cliffs, it has an atmosphere more completely marine than almost any other part of this coast, with the exception, of course, of St. Leonards, which possesses the same dry and absorbent soil.

The breadth and extent of its esplanade, also, and the protection afforded by the colonnades for walking exercise, are circumstances of considerable importance to the invalid, and render a conjoined residence at Hastings and St Leonards a very efficient substitute for a trip to Madeira.

The Castle of Hastings, for a time the favourite residence of the Conqueror, has remained a mass of magnificent ruins; its towers, bastions, and ancient walls forming an object truly picturesque, as seen from any point of view, but looking even grand in their sombre desolation, as meeting the eye of the pedestrian when ascending the eminence leading to Fairlight Downs.

A few years back the visitors to the castle were shown two coffins, a small one and a larger one, which they were assured contained the ashes of a mother and infant. These have been lately removed, and the space of ground enclosed by the walls which used to shelter such vestiges of a more barbarous age is now employed by a market gardener to administer to the culinary wants of the townsfolk of Hastings and St Leonards.

The approach to Hastings Castle is from the further extremity of Wellington Square, and, with the perpendicular cliff that fronts the sea for its base, the outer walls appear originally to have had the form of a triangle with rounded angles. For some time past

1066 and all that

1066 is a date seared into the memory of every schoolchild. The castle at Hastings was founded by William the Conqueror in 1070. Other attractions include the caves, two funicular railways, the old town and traditional seaside entertainments. It still has a pier, on which restoration has just commenced following the fire which nearly destroyed it in October 2010. *(Simon Jeffs)*

Bradshaw makes several references to Martello towers. These are small defensive forts built in various parts of the British Empire, but most notably along the south and east coast. Their inspiration comes from sixteenth-century defences at Mortella in Corsica, and the circular design was modified for the chain of 103 towers constructed between 1804 and 1812 to defend against possible invasion from Napoleon's forces. No. 74, shown left, is at Seaford. *(Poliphilo)*

the interior has been laid out as a flower garden and shrubbery, and the person who has charge of the lodge accommodates, for a small fee, visitors with seats and refreshments. The view, though not equal to that from Fairlight Downs, is varied and extensive, and commands towards the south an ample marine expanse, whilst Beachy Head, Eastbourne, and Bexhill may be seen towards the west.

Whilst in the neighbourhood, it should not be forgotten that a delightful excursion may be made to Battle Abbey, not more than six miles distant. The grounds are now in possession of the Webster family, who have liberally thrown them open to public inspection every Friday, at 1.30 p.m. It is here that the 'Battel Roll,' a sort of primitive 'Court Guide,' is carefully preserved, and furnishes a list valuable to the antiquary and historian of those families who came over with William the Conqueror.

A glance into the booksellers' windows, where engraved vignettes of some neighbouring attraction allure the eye in every direction, will at once reveal to the visitor the tempting beauty of the environs. A week may be delightfully spent in exploring the fairy-like nooks about Fairlight alone. Situated in a sweet umbrageous spot, down which, by narrow winding steps, hewn out of the solid rock, one only can descend at a time, is the weeping rock. The view of this constantly-dripping well, as the spectator looks up to the jutting rock from the beautiful cottage of Covehurst below, is well calculated to inspire the mind with that feeling under which credence would be given to any legend that accounted for this freak of nature, by ascribing it to the influence of supernatural agency. The stone weeps, as it were, from myriads of pores, and, although the water falls in continuous drops, no trace of it is left in the reservoir; passing through the rock, its appearance is as mysterious as its disappearance is magical. It is explained by the soil beneath being loose and sandy, over a heavy beach stone foundation, and, acting as a subterraneous drain, the water is conducted beneath the surface, appearing as a truculent stream about a hundred yards from the rock, and then again disappearing down a declivity. The beautiful appearance the rock presents in winter, when the drip is frozen and the icicles hang from the sloping crags in clusters of crystals, will not be easily forgotten by those who have had the good fortune to witness, at this period, such a mimic stalactite cavern.

Then, in the vicinity of the well are the fish-ponds with romantic walks around it, and a comfortable farm-house adjacent, where refreshments can he had at a small cost, and where the ale is – but we forbear our eloquence. The picturesque waterfall of Old Roar should not be overlooked, nor the Lover's Seat, so charmingly enthroned amid shrubs and evergreens, nor the other favoured localities, which are enough to make a Pennsylvanian lawyer turn poetical. Let the pedestrian, however, make his way to the signal house belonging to the coast-guard station at that point, and he will have a panoramic view around him which it would be worth his while walking from Cornhill to Grand Cairo only to behold and then walk back again.

The whole forms a complete circle; the sweep of inland scenery extending to the hills in the neighbourhood of London, and the sea view reaching from Beachy Head to Dover Cliffs, between seventy and eighty miles apart, and stretching out to the heights of Boulogne. The entire area of the prospect, both by land and water, cannot be less than three hundred miles. Among many minor objects visible may be enumerated ten towns,

Winchelsea

Above: Winchelsea is a relatively new town as the original was swallowed by the waves in 1287. Once a port, the sea is now several miles away. It is considered to be the smallest town in England. *(Laurel Anison)*

Rye

Left: Rightly regarded as one of the most beautiful towns in the country, Rye has a long seafaring history and was one of the 'Antient Townes' (Winchelsea being the other). It became a limb of the Cinque Ports Confederation in 1189, and subsequently a full member. The SER line from Ashford opened in 1850 and from Hastings in 1851. Despite several attempts to close the line, it retains an hourly service that runs from Brighton to Ashford. The original station building, *bottom left,* is still in use. *(Fred Matthews)*

sixty-six churches, seventy Martello towers, five ancient castles, three bays, and forty windmills. The best time for seeing it is the afternoon, when the setting sun lights up the old town of Hastings in the foreground, and firings into strong shadow the opposite coast of France. Upon favourable atmospheric influences it is, indeed, a view never to be forgotten.

[On the eastern extreme of Sussex the line from Ashford to Hastings crosses the border from Kent to Rye and Winchelsea.]

RYE

Population, 8,202. A telegraph station. Hotel – George. Omnibuses to Peasmarsh, Beckley, Northiam, Newenden, Rolvenden, and Benenden. Market Days – Wednesday (Corn), Saturday (Meal), and every Wednesday fortnight (Stock).
Fairs – Whit-Monday and August 10th. Money Order Office. Bankers – Curteis, Pomfret, Pix, Billingham & Pix. Branch of London & County Bank.

Rye, a borough town in the county of Sussex. It stands on an eminence near the mouth of the river Rother. In the reign of Edward III, Rye sent nine armed vessels to the royal fleet when that monarch invaded France. In the next reign it was burnt and plundered by the French. From this and other unfavourable circumstances, the town remained for many years in a state of great decay, but its prosperity has in a great measure been restored.

WINCHELSEA

Distance from station, 1 1/2 mile. A telegraph station. Hotel – New Inn. Passenger vans to Hastings. Market Day – Sat. Fair – May 14th (Cattle). Money Order Office at Rye.

The original sea port, which bore its name, was swallowed up by the sea on the eve of St Agatha, 1287, and although the buildings were then erected further inland, the sea, unappeased by the former sacrifice, broke in anew, and finally, in the time of Queen Elizabeth, altogether choked up the harbour. The ruins of the castle of Ounber, built by Henry VIII, are still standing, and so are three out of the four gates, but they are in a ruinous condition.

London & South Western Railway

When it opened for business in 1848, the Waterloo Bridge station, as it was known, was only intended to be another station on the line extending from Nine Elms to a point in more central London. As a result it expanded in a piecemeal fashion and it was in 1899 that the LSWR decided upon a total rebuild. In the event this was not completed until 1922 and consequently there is little of the present station that Bradshaw would recognise. The postcard shown above is from around 1905. *Below:* Something definitely from Bradshaw's era, *Nelson* is a 2-4-0WT, designed by the LSWR's chief engineer Joseph Beattie, of the eponymous Nelson class of 18158. *(CMcC)*

Surrey

LONDON AND SOUTH WESTERN

The main branches of this railway communicate with the suburbs of London, and are mostly celebrated for their picturesque beauty, viz.: Richmond, Windsor, Kew, and the valley of the Thames, Hampton Court, Kingston, Claremont, Guildford, etc.; also with Portsmouth, Winchester, Southampton, Salisbury, Isle of Wight, and Weymouth, via Dorchester.

Of all the many alluring rambles held forth to the tourist who wishes to avail himself of the speedy communication by rail with some of the most picturesque scenery in England, there is no line that possesses more intrinsic advantages, or which intersects in its various routes so many places of glorious memory as the South Western, from the metropolis to the south-western coast of Hampshire and Devonshire.

The metropolitan terminus of the South Western is at Waterloo Road. Omnibuses convey passengers to and from all parts of town. The terminus is a spacious building, admirably adapted for the different railway offices and the various departments connected with the Company. The gentle pace at which the trains first move afford time for observing the extensive engine houses and workshops at Nine Elms. The line passes over viaducts or arches through a part of the densely populated parish of Lambeth, over the tops of houses, past the grounds of Lambeth Palace, in a line with which is Lambeth Church, and across the river may be seen the splendid towers of the new Houses of Parliament.

SURREY

This is one of the most interesting, if not the most fertile, of the English counties. Almost the whole surface of the county is undulating, and consists of hill and dale, intersecting each other in, every variety of form. In some parts extensive heaths give an air of wildness to the prospect which is strikingly contrasted by the innumerable beauties scattered over the surface of the county by the hand of art, while the hills, which frequently approach the height of mountains, decline into richly wooded dales and plains, covered with luxuriant harvests. In many parts the landscapes are diversified with picturesque uplands, romantic heights, woodland dells, verdant valleys, and plains covered with waving com. The most striking feature of the county, however, is its extensive chalky downs, lying nearly in the centre. The railway communications of the county are numerous, and intersect it in all directions.

MAIN LINE – LONDON TO CLAPHAM

VAUXHALL

A telegraph station. Steam vessels to London Bridge, and Chelsea, Pimlico, Fulham, Battersea, Wandsworth, Putney, Richmond, Kew, and Hammersmith Bridge (calling at all the piers on the banks of the river), every five minutes.

Money Order Office, No. 4, Wandsworth Road.

Thence we pass on through Vauxhall, and entering upon an embankment bounded on each side by spacious market gardens, the line passes Battersea New Town and park on the one hand, and Battersea Rise and Clapham on the other, at which point the, Richmond, Staines, and Windsor line diverges to the right, while the main line turns off towards the left to Wimbledon.

As the Richmond and Windsor railway is the first branch of the South Western, we will commence our description with that.

Windsor and Richmond branch

Wandsworth to Barnes

The Richmond line properly branches off about the point where the road to the village of Battersea leaves the Wandsworth road, and at a short distance from Battersea. It then pursues a pretty course through the villas, orchards, and nursery gardens which stud that locality, till it reaches Wandsworth. The river Wandle and the valley arc crossed by a splendid viaduct.

WANDSWORTH

Telegraph station at Vauxhall, 8 miles.

This station, situated within a short distance of the parish that gives it the name of Wandsworth, which with the other suburban districts we have passed through, contains a number of elegant villas, belonging to the opulent class of city merchants. On leaving Wandsworth we have for a moment a picturesque peep at the Thames, and the line pursues a southerly direction through a deep cutting of some extent, until we reach

PUTNEY

Telegraph station at Barnes, 1 1/4 mile. Omnibuses to London, via Fulham, Chelsea, and Brampton, every quarter of an hour. Steamboats – To London every hour, calling at the different Piers on the river side, and to Richmond, Hammersmith, and Kew, daily, in summer.

On emerging from the cutting and passing this station, we proceed over a level country to Barnes Common, which the line crosses.

BARNES

> Distance from station, 1/2 mile. A telegraph station.
>
> Money Order Office at Hammersmith.

Barnes is memorable, among other associations, as being the place where Sir Francis Walsingham entertained Queen Elizabeth and her retinue, at an enormous expense, though the next year he died at his house in Seething Lane so poor, that his friends were obliged to bury him privately at night. The church, about a quarter of a mile from the river, is one of the most ancient in the neighbourhood of the metropolis, having been erected in the reign of Richard I (1189). Here lived Jacob Tonson, the bookseller, the founder and secretary of the Kit-Cat Club.

Loop Line

BAMES TO HOUNSLOW AND FELTHAM

It diverges from the Richmond line at Barnes station, and is carried across the river Thames, in front of Barnes-terrace, by means of a light and elegant bridge, consisting of three arches. From this the line proceeds through the property of the Duke of Devonshire; and the first station, Chiswick, is placed at the southernmost corner of his Grace's park. This station, besides accommodating the residents, is within a very short distance of the Horticultural Society's Gardens, and is one of the principal means of approach on *fete* and other days. The railway then passes on to Kew Bridge, where it crosses the turnpike road.

KEW

> Population, 1,102. Distance from station, 1/2 mile. A telegraph station.
>
> Hotels – Coach & Horses; Rose & Crown; Star & Garter.
>
> Omnibuses to and from the station; also every five minutes to and from London.
>
> Steam Boats to London, frequently during the day in summer.
>
> Money Order Office at Brentford, 1 1/2 mile.

Kew, a picturesque village on the banks of the Thames, about seven miles from London, and one mile from Richmond. The palace contains a few pictures, but the gardens are the principal objects of attraction. They are not very large, nor is their situation advantageous, as it is low and commands no prospects; but they contain the finest collection of plants in this country, and are decorated with various ornamental buildings, The first which appears is the orangery, or green-house, Near it, in a grove, is the temple of the Sun, of the Corinthian order. There is also a medico-botanical garden, and contiguous to it, the flower garden, of which the principal entrance forms one end. The two sides are enclosed with high trees, and the other end is occupied by an aviary of vast depth. From the flower garden, a short winding walk leads to the menagerie, the centre of which is occupied by a large basin of water, originally stocked

Completed in 1848, the Palm House at Kew was a cooperation between architect Decimus Burton and the iron founder Richard Turner. *(Jim)*

with curious water-fowl, and enclosed by a range of cages of exotic birds. The gardens also contain the temples of Bellona, the gods Pan, Aeolus, Solitude, and Victory, the House of Confucius and the great Pagoda, 165 feet high, from the top of which is an extensive view of a rich and variegated country. The Palm House is one of the finest in Europe; it cost upwards of £30,000. The royal pleasure grounds are open to the public on Thursdays and Sundays, from Midsummer until Michaelmas. The Botanic Gardens are also open every day from one till six.

> So sits enthroned in vegetable pride
> Imperial Kew, by Thames's glistening side,
> Obedient sails from realms unfurrow'd bring
> For her the unnamed progeny of spring.'

From this point the line passes principally through market gardens to Boston Lane, where the Brentford station is conveniently placed.

BRENTFORD

Population, 9,521. Distance from station ½ mile. A telegraph station.
Hotels – Red Lion; George IV. Omnibuses to and from London, Inglefield Green, Egham, and Isleworth. Market Days – Tuesdays. Fairs – May 17th, 18th, and 19th; Sept. 12th, 13th, and 14th. Bankers – Branch of London & County Bank.

Brentford has a weekly market and two annual fairs. It is the county town, where members of Parliament are elected. Here the Brent falls into the Thames. The town is a long straggling street.

ISLEWORTH

Distance from station, 3/4 mile. Telegraph station at Brentford, mile.

Fairs – First Monday in July. Money Order Office at Hounslow.

Isleworth, with its picturesque ivy-mantled church tower, was noted for affording excellent sport to anglers. The salmon caught in this part of the Thames was formerly of a peculiarly fine quality, but the gas works and steam navigation have driven them higher up the stream. This place, however, is still frequented by anglers, who consider there is not finer fishing anywhere than in the Thames from Kew to Richmond.

Sion House, the magnificent edifice of the Duke of Somerset, where Lady Jane Grey resided, now belonging to the Duke of Northumberland, was built here, on the site of a suppressed nunnery. The grounds form a fine lawn, extending from Brentford to Isleworth.

HOUNSLOW

Population, 5,760. Distance from station, 1 mile. Telegraph station at Brentford, 3 miles. Hotel – George. Omnibuses to and from Harlington and London, daily. Fairs – Trinity Monday and Monday after Michaelmas Day.

Richmond Branch continued

BARNES TO WINDSOR

A great portion of the line is but a few feet above the natural surface, of the country, and many of the roads arc crossed on a level. The country through which it passes docs not present many picturesque views, the property almost throughout being circumscribed by orchards and market gardens. The want, however, of the beautiful along the line is amply compensated by the lovely views in the neighbourhood of Richmond; and from Richmond to Datchet there is a succession of splendid scenery.

The first station at which' we arrive is

MORTLAKE

Telegraph station at Richmond, 1 1/2 mile. Inn – Kings Arms.

Money Order Office at Richmond.

The remainder of the course is through fields and gardens, passing a little to the south of the grounds of Kew, or to the terminus in the Kew Road at Richmond.

RICHMOND

Population, 7,423. Distance from station, 1/2 mile.

A telegraph station. Hotels – Star & Garter; Roebuck; Castle.

Omnibuses to and from the station; also to London, via Kew, Hammersmith, and Kensington; conveyances also to Hampton, Kingston, and Twickenham. These are

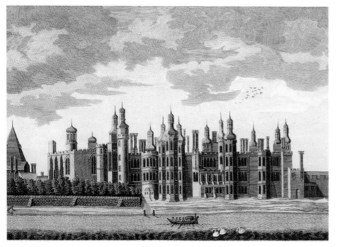

Richmond

Bradshaw describes Richmond as 'a delightful town in Surrey, on the South Western Railway and the river Thames'. Richmond remained part of the county until the mid-1960s.

Top left: A view of Richmond Palace published in 1765. The pyramid on the far left is the roof of the Great Kitchen. The palace was the first building in England to have a flushing toilet. Only vestiges of the palace now remain.

Left: Postcard view of the bridge at Richmond, *c.* 1910. *(CMcC)*

Below: A later postcard showing George Street in Richmond. *(CMcC)*

the fastest and best appointed vehicles out of London. Vessels from London, calling at Putney, Hammersmith Bridge, and Kew, daily in summer.

Richmond is a delightful town in Surrey, on the South Western Railway and the river Thames, 10 miles from London, in the midst of scenery which, though often praised and admired, never grows old or wearisome. It may he also reached by the omnibus from St Paul's, every hour and half hour, or by the Hampton Court steamer from London and Hungerford Bridges. The last way is the best for enjoying the scenery of the river above Richmond; but the shoals and the long bends or readies make it rather tedious, especially at low tides. The town stands on an eminence on the south hank of the Thames – it extends about a mile up the hill – and is skirted and intermingled with agreeable gardens.

Richmond had a royal palace from the time of Edward I, called *Sheen*, ie. Shining, till Henry VII gave it the title which he bore as Earl of Richmond, borrowed from his castle of that name in Yorkshire, and revived by Charles I for the ancestor of the Lennox family. Both places are seated on a high point, 'Richce-mont', overlooking a vast range of country. A brick gate and some old walls on one side of the Green are the solo remnants of the *palace*, which Henry VIII gave to Wolsey in exchange for Hampton Court, but as it soon returned to the crown it became the residence of Elizabeth, who died here in 1603, and of Henrietta Maria, the queen of Charles I. On the green in front tournaments were held before Henry VII and Henry VIII. This place is also noted for having had the earliest calico print works established in it (1696) by a Frenchman – these have since thriven in a more congenial spot The old park was behind the palace, and now makes part of Kew Gardens; the great park, on the top of the hill, was not enclosed till Charles I's time. In ascending to it you pass the brick church in which Thomson the poet, Mrs Yates, and Kean the actors, Dr Moore the author of *Zelnco* and father of Sir John Moore, are burried; it contains also Flaxman's monument of Mrs Lowther. Thomson died at *Rosedale House*, now the Dowager Countess of Shaftesbury's seat, and here his desk, garden sent, etc. are to be seen. The sight of the church put Collins in mind of writing his pretty lines on him, beginning, 'In yonder shade a Druid lies'. At the top of the hill, half a mile from the town, where Sir J. Reynolds's house stands, you catch the splendid prospect so often celebrated:

> Thy hill, delightful *Shene*! Here let us sweep
> The boundless landscape. Now the raptured eye
> Exulting, swift to huge Augusta send,
> Now to the sister hills that skirt her plain,
> To lofty Harrow bow, and now to where
> Majestic Windsor lifts his princely brow.
>
> Slow let us trace the matchless vale of Thames;
> Fair winding-up to where the muses haunt
> In Twit'ham's bowers – to Royal Hampton's pile,
> To Claremont's terraced heights and Esher's groves.
>
> *Thomson*

It would be worthwhile to read the noble lines which follow this quotation in the poet's 'Summer', sitting under elms on this spot; there is a glow and dignity in them equal to the magnificence of the prospect spread out before one's eyes. The great lodge which was Sir R. Walpole's seat, *Pembroke Lodge*, the seat of Earl Russell, the *New Terrace*, offer some of the best points of view in the park. The Marquis of Lansdowne, the mansion now owned bythe Duchess of Gloucester, formerly the seat of Lord Sidmouth, called the *Ranger's Lodge*, and many more, have houses on or round the hill.

The Wesleyan body have a college here for the theological students – a handsome Tudor range, 250 feet long, in which is a good statue of their founder. Close to the bridge (built in 1747, and still taxed) are three small aits or wooded islands. The railway viaduct strides across the three wide arches below.

Within a few miles are kew gardens and its pagoda; Twickenham, the favourite retreat of Pope; East Sheen, where Sir W. Temple lived. Ham, the ancient seat of the Dysart family, in which the famous John, Duke of Argyle was born (Scott, in his Heart of Mid Lothian, brings him to Richmond park, to introduce Jeannie Deans to Queen Caroline), and Hampton Court, with its half Tudor, half French palace, pictures, cartoons, lely beauties, gardens, and other attractions.

The line crosses the Thames over the railway bridge at Richmond – a very handsome structure of three arches.

[The line continues to Twickenham in the county of Middlesex and re-enters Surrey at Egham]

STAINES TO WOKINGHAM AND READING

On leaving Staines we soon arrive at

EGHAM

Telegraph station at Staines, 2 miles. Hotels – Crown, Victoria Arms, Coach and Horses. Races (at Runnymede) in August.

The church contains tombs of Abbot John of Chertsey, and Sir J. Denham, father of the poet.

In the vicinity are *Egham Lodge*, seat of J. Dobinson, Esq.: *Kingswood Lodge*, Mrs Read. Runnymede (½ mile), memorable as the Council Meadow, where the English Barons compelled King John to sign the Magna Charta on Trinity Monday, 15th June, 1215. *Runnymede House*, seat of N. Reid, Esq.; *Cooper's Hill*, so beautifully described by the poet Denham. We then pass along two miles of beautiful scenery and reach ...

VIRGINIA WATER

Telegraph station at Sunningdale, 4 miles. Hotel – Wheatsheaf.

This beautiful lake, situated in Windsor Forest, was planned by the Duke of Cumberland, above 100 years ago. Open daily to the public. It is the largest piece of artificial water in the kingdom, if that can be called artificial where man has only collected the streams of the district into a natural basin. The surrounding scenery is exceedingly pleasing and picturesque. After passing through a woody dell, we come to some serpentine walks, which lead in different directions; those to the right conducting us to a somewhat steep hill, on the summit of which stands a handsome Gothic battlemented building, called *Belvidere*; and those to the left leading to the margin of the lake. At the head of the lake is a cascade, descending some twenty feet, over massive fragments of stone, into a dark glen or ravine. Near it is an obelisk standing on a small mount, and bearing the following inscription, added by William IV:

> This obelisk was raised by the command of George II., after the battle of Culloden, in commemoration of the services of his son William, Duke of Cumberland, the success of his arms, and the gratitude of his father.

There is a road hence to the banks of the lake, where we can reach a rustic bridge, and get a fine view of the waterfall and its cavern adjacent, formed of stone brought from Bagshot Heath, where they indicated the ruins of a Saxon cromlech. At the point where the lake is widest, a fishing temple was erected by George IV.

A bold arch carries the public road to Blacknest, over a portion of the grounds, and adjoining is an ornamental ruin, called the 'Temple of the Gods', manufactured from some really antique fragments of Greek columns and pediments, that used to life in the courtyard of the British Museum. The effect is striking, and much more so if the spectator will for a moment let fancy delude him into the belief that he is gazing on a real temple of ancient Athens. The tall trees, clustering round in one part, and in another opening on to glades of truly sylvan aspect, impart a romantic beauty to the landscape from tins point, which utterly defies description. It is worthwhile to cross the little bridge above al¬luded to, and, passing one of the streams that feed the lake, pursue its windings among the underwood, or strike into the path which leads to Bishopsgate, a beautiful village, environed by all the charms of wood and water diversity. Here resided for some time Shelley, who has consecrated the allurements of this spot by some of his finest poems, written in the vicinity. There are several ways of approaching Virginia Water, each so attractive that it is difficult to decide upon the best; but, by whichever route the excursionist comes, we would suggest the adoption of another road for the return. About two miles beyond the town of Egham is a neat wayside inn, called the Wheatsheaf, from the garden of which there is direct access to the lake. From Egham Hill a road diverges through Windsor Park to Reading, nineteen miles distant. A few hundred yards above the inn is a branch road to the right, leading to Blacknest, where there is also an entrance through the keeper's lodge. Beside this, there is a delightful drive of five miles to Virginia Water from Chertsey.

SOUTH WESTERN MAIN LINE – CLAPHAM TO KINGSTON

Soon after rejoining the Main Line at Clapham Common, a branch to the left leads to the Crystal Palace, via Balharn, Streatham, and Norwood.

CLAPHAM

Population, 20,894. Distance from station, 1 mile. A telegraph station.
Money Order Office No. 2, Holland Place, Clapham.

Wimbledon Park, the seat of the Earl Spencer, is seen to the right; thence crossing the old Surrey Railway, we at the same time pass over Garratt Lane, the little village adjoining, which was formerly the scene of a mock election, rendered popular by Foote's grotesque farce of the Mayor of Garratt.

The adjacent country now begins to assume a very pleasant and diversified appearance, and the patches of woodland scenery that break forth in bold relief; against the distant horizon furnish an agreeable foretaste of the picturesque views yet to come. Passing beneath a few arches which connect the roads leading from various adjacent' villages, we reach the station at

WIMBLEDON

Distance from station, 1/4 mile. A telegraph station. Hotel – Rose and Crown.

Wimbledon was formerly celebrated in the annals of duelling, a practice which has now become synonymous with our notions of *'such killing being murder'*, and therefore, like many other customs and habits of uncivilised beings, it has been discountenanced and condemned by that general spirit of good feeling and sense which now happily pervades all classes of the community.

Merton – Distance from the Wimbledon station, 3/4 mile; Telegraph station at Wimbledon, 5 mile. Hotel – White Hart. The pretty village of Merton, where Lord Nelson lived, is a favourite resort of excursionists.

Croydon Branch

WIMBLEDON TO CROYDON

This is a short line connecting the South Eastern and Southern with the Western Counties; the stations being Morden, Mitcham, Beddington, Croydon.

Leatherhead Branch

WIMBLEDON TO EPSOM AND LEATHERHEAD

This branch is intended subsequently to unite with the London and Portsmouth Direct, at Godalming, via Epsom. At present it is opened to Leatherhead, about half-way. The stations en route from Wimbledon are Old Malden, Ewell, the church of which has some curious monuments, Epsom, Ashstead – Ashtead Park, the seat of Colonel Howard.

LEATHERHEAD

A telegraph station. Hotels – Swan; Duke's Head. Fair – Oct. 10th, horses and pigs.

This place is situated on the river Mole. The church was built about the year 1346, in the form of a cross, but has since been restored.

An excursion may be made from here to Stoke d'Abernon (3 1/2 miles), passing through Woodlands Park, the seat of J. Smith, Esq. The old church (St Mary's), at *Stoke d'Abernon* (or Alborne), lies embedded in trees, close to the Manor House (Rev. F. Parr Phillips). It contains the most ancient monumental brasses in England, and is much resorted to by antiquarians. The two most celebrated brasses to the D'Abernon family are in the chancel. The church also contains a curious hour-glass and stand, and is otherwise interesting. The key is at the Manor House.

South Western Main Line continued.

SURBITON TO WEYBRIDGE

ESHER

A telegraph station.

This is the nearest station for Esher and Claremont; the former, once a place of some importance, is now little better than an inconsiderable Village. Esher Place is remarkable as having been the residence of Wolsey, when Bishop of Winchester; and a small castled turret, near the River Mole, is exhibited as the place of his temporary imprisonment.

Claremont, which is adjoining, has a melancholy interest, from the death of the lamented Princess Charlotte, which took place in 1817. The palace has since belonged to her husband, the King of the Belgians, who subsequently appropriated it to the use of the exiled Orleans family, when Louis Philippe left France in 1848, and who have resided in it since his death, in comparative seclusion.

From the Ditton station we cross Walton Heath, and reach the station at

WALTON & HERSHAM

A telegraph station. Distance from station, 1 mile to either place. Hotels – (Walton) Duke's Head; Castle Inn. Fairs – Wednesday and Thursday in Easter Week.

The Walton station is a short distance from Hersham, one mile to the left, and the same distance from Walton to the right. In the old church of St Mary's, which may be seen rising amongst the trees, will be found various interesting monuments of considerable antiquity. A 'scold bridle' is shown. *Apps Court*, near Walton, was another of the many residences once belonging to Wolsey; and *Ashley Park*, the seat of the Fletcher family, is memorable for having been the temporary abode of Cromwell, prior to his assuming the Protectorate. Emerging from the Walton cutting we gain a somewhat lofty embankment, affording some picturesque views, through which the translucent Wey meanders like a glistening thread.

WEYBRIDGE

Distance from station, 3/4 mile. A telegraph station. Hotels – Hand and Spear, Ship.

Here is a commodious hotel adjoining the station, with some extensive grounds. The scenery in this neighbourhood is beautiful, and St George's Hill commands a delightful view of Windsor, Richmond, and Chertsey,

A little distance beyond Weybridge station a short line branches off to Addlestone and Chertsey.

Chertsey Branch

WEYBRIDGE TO CHERTSEY

Addlestone station.

CHERTSEY

Distance from station, 1/2 mile. Telegraph, station at Weybridge, 31/4 miles.
Hotel – Swan. Market Day – Wednesday. Fairs – First Monday in Lent, May 14th,
August 6th, and September 25th.

Chertsey is as old as the days of the ancient Britons, and probably was one of their principal places. Soon after the conversion of the Saxons from Paganism, in 666, a Benedictine monastery was founded here by Frithwald, a petty prince of Surrey, and by him richly endowed. In the original charter it is written, 'I beseech those whose names are annexed to subscribe themselves witnesses that I, Frithwald, who am the giver, together with the Abbot Erkenwald, on account of my ignorance of letters, have expressed with the sign of the Holy Cross.' It is from this pretty evident that princes in those days had somewhat of Jack Cade's antipathy to those who could 'read, write, and cast accompt', and therefore they also 'made their mark, like a simple, plain-dealing, honest man'. The Danes, who were the general 'snappers-up of unconsidered trifles,' pillaged the abbey in 1009, killed the abbot and monks, and laid the whole building desolate; but being afterwards rebuilt by Egbert, King of Kent, it became more magnificently embellished than ever, and was one of the most important monasteries in the kingdom. Henry VI was buried here, under a sumptuous mausoleum, but the body was exhumed in 1504, by Henry VII, and conveyed with great pomp, first to Windsor, and afterwards to Westminster Abbey. It is useless to look now for any vestige of its former grandeur; all that remains is a part of its wall, forming the boundary of an orchard, and part of an archway is still visible on the north side of the town. In the centre of the town is the chinch, rebuilt in 1808, but having a portion of the old chancel and lower remaining. Even so late as the year 1814, and occasionally since, the curfew has been tolled here, from Michaelmas to Lady-day, the day of the month being indicated during the time of ringing. A handsome stone bridge of seven arches was erected, in 1786, across the Thames, connecting the counties of Surrey and Middlesex. At a house in Guildford Street, formerly distinguished as the Porch House, lived Abraham Cowley, the poet, who has perpetuated, in prose and verse, his love for this seclusion in a hundred quaint prettinesses. Beneath the window of the room in which he died (July 28th, 1667) is a tablet thus appealing to the sympathies of the passers-by, 'Hero the last accents flowed from Cowley's tongue.' A pretty summer house that he built, and a seat under a sycamore tree, both mentioned in his poems, were existing till the middle of the last century. After the excursionist has refreshed his physical energies at one of the many excellent inns that here abound, by all moans let him ascend St Anne's Hill, about a mile out of tile town, and he shall find himself, at the summit, elevated some 250 feet above the ocean level, with a glorious panorama round about him of the finest parts-of the river between Richmond and Windsor. There is a spring at the top, that summer's heat and winter's cold alike prove unable to dry up or freeze. The mansion on the southern slope of the hill was once the residence of Charles James Fox, the statesman, to whom a cenotaph has been erected in the church.

South Western Main Line continued

From the hill before Weybridge to Woking, a distance of six miles, there is a gradual descent Alter crossing the bridge which spans the Basingstoke Canal, here intersected by the canal from Guildford, and passing several villages, we pass over the Woking embankment, whence a succession of picturesque views will delight the traveller. Ottershaw Park affords a pleasing specimen of English forest scenery. The fine effect of these majestic trees, with nothing behind them but the sunny splendour of a summer morning, or the rich glow of an evening, sky, realises all that Claude has embodied in his pictures.

WOKING

Distance from station, 1 mile. A telegraph station. Hotels – White Hart; Railway.
Fair – Whit Tuesday.

On both sides of the line Woking Common is seen to extend for miles, only broken by the windings of the Basingstoke Canal, and terminated by a long range of woodland scenery, which stands out in picturesque relief against the horizon.

Three-quarters of a mile beyond Woking a line branches off to the left to Guildford and Godalming, direct to Portsmouth, from which another branch diverges at Guildford, and extends to Ash, Farnham, and Alton.

Guildford.—Particulars will be found on page 87.

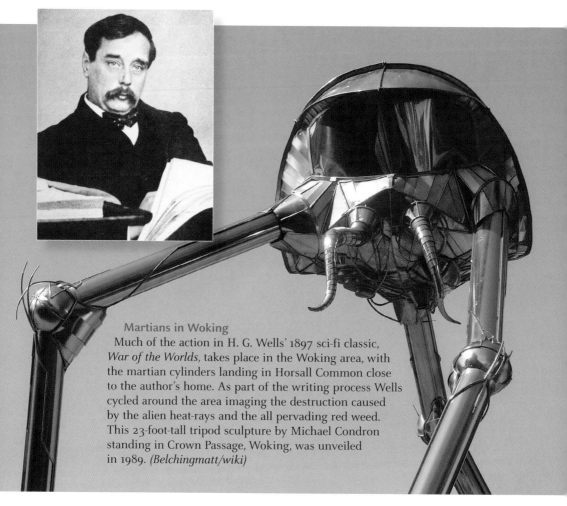

Martians in Woking

Much of the action in H. G. Wells' 1897 sci-fi classic, *War of the Worlds*, takes place in the Woking area, with the martian cylinders landing in Horsall Common close to the author's home. As part of the writing process Wells cycled around the area imaging the destruction caused by the alien heat-rays and the all pervading red weed. This 23-foot-tall tripod sculpture by Michael Condron standing in Crown Passage, Woking, was unveiled in 1989. *(Belchingmatt/wiki)*

Above left: Built in 1889, the Shah Jahan Mosque in Woking was the first purpose-built example in the UK. Also known as the Woking Mosque, the Grade II* building is still in use. *(CMcC)*

Above right: Postcard view of the High Street in Godalming. *(CMcC)*

Alton Branch

GUILDFORD TO ALTON

ASH

Distance from station, 1 mile. A telegraph station. Money Order Office – at Farnham.

Tongham station for Aldershot.

FARNHAM

Population, 3,926. Distance from station, 5 miles. A telegraph station.
Hotel – Bush. Market Days – Thursdays. Fairs – Holy Thursday, June 24th, November 13th, October 10th. Bankers – John & James Knight.

Farnham contains much to interest the tourist. Putting its celebrity for hops out of the question, there is the old castle; which has been the seat of the bishops of Winchester since the time of King Stephen, and the neighbourhood abounds with vestiges of former monastic splendour. The exquisitely beautiful ruins of Waverley Abbey, about a mile from the town, are alone a reward for any pilgrimage that may be made from the station. It has the earliest Cistercian foundation in England. *Moore Park* was the seat of Temple, whose heart was buried in a silver box under the sun-dial. Swift was his secretary at the time, and here wrote his correspondence with Stella.

[Beyond Farnham the line crosses the border into Hampshire and continues south-westwards to Bentley and Alton.]

GODALMING

Population, 2,321. Distance from station, 1/4 mile. A telegraph station.
Hotel – King's Arms. Market Day – Wednesday. Fairs – February 13th, and July 10th. Bankers – Mellersh & Keen.

This town is situated on the banks of the Wye, at a point where that river divides into several streams; it is a considerable trading and manufacturing town. The manufactures are stocking weaving of all kinds, fleecy hosiery, blankets, worsteds, cotton cloths, etc. It consists of a principal street, running cast and west, and several smaller ones; the church is much admired and has a handsome spire.

Croydon–Epsom Branch

CARSHALTON

Distance from station, 3/4 mile. A telegraph station. Hotels – Greyhound, King's Arms. Fairs – July 1st and 2nd. Money Order Office at Carshalton.

Epsom

Noted for 'Epsom Salts' (magnesium sulphate derived from its mineral springs) and the racecourse where the famous Derby Stakes, Britain's richest horse race, is held annually on the first Saturday in June. This has always been a big occasion, with a huge audience thronging the Epsom Downs. Once the railways arrived in Epsom in 1847 crowds the could walk across the Downs to the racecourse. Epsom station is shown top left in 1865, and more recently, *left*. *(SEG archives)* Later, both the SER and LBSCR built stations to serve the racecourse at Tattenham Corner, bottom left *(Colin Scott-Morton)* and Epsom Downs, respectively. Race traffic is now concentrated at Tattenham Corner, but this is a shadow of its former glory.

Above: A charming hand-painted postcard depicting Edward VII examining the form at Epsom. *(CMcC)*

Sutton, Cheam, and Ewell Stations.

EPSOM

A Population, 4,890. A telegraph station. Hotel – Spread Eagle.
Market Day – Wednesday. Fair – July 25th.
Races in April, September, and week before Whitsuntide.

This place is interesting in many points of view, but more especially for its celebrated race-course. It is on the west side of Banstead Downs. During the race week Epsom has the appearance of a busy crowded city; and if the weather be fine, there are seldom less than 60,000 persons assembled here on the great day when the Derby Stakes arc contested. The distance was done by Surplice, in 1848, in two minutes forty-eight seconds. Epsom is famous for its mineral spring, from which Epsom salts (sulphate of magnesia) is prepared.

Returning to Croydon we will now pass over the

Croydon–Wimbledon Branch

CROYDON TO WIMBLEDON

The first stations being Beddington and Mitcham, both on the river Wandle. The church of the latter is worth a visit. We then approach the station of Morden, near which is Merton, possessing much historical interest. Here are the remains of a rich abbey founded for St Augustine Canons; and here Ethelred I was defeated by the Danes, 871, and received his death wound. Here were enacted 'the provisions of Merton,' in the reign of Henry III; and here the glorious Nelson lived. The church is partly of Norman, and partly of the early English styles. Morden Park, 1⁄2 mile.

Caterham Branch

SOUTH EASTERN RAILWAY

This branch, the length of which is 4 5/8 miles, turns off to the left from Caterham Junction, and passes the stations of Kenley and Warlingham. The line runs through the valley of Caterham, the country about which is hilly, and beautifully diversified.

CATERHAM

A telegraph station. Hotel – Railway.

The village itself does not possess anything worthy of notice; but. there are extensive stone quarries about 1 1⁄2 mile, distant, the quality of which material being well adapted for building, will in all probability cause many villas and residences to be erected here.

Caterham

The branch line from Caterham Junction (now Purley) was opened to this small Surrey town in 1862. The commemorative plaque, *left*, marks the 150th anniversary of this nice little station which is used by commuters to London and Croydon.

Below: Caterham station photographed in 2014. *(Simon Jeffs)*

Left: To the petrol-heads of this world, the name Caterham is forever associated with the iconic Caterham 7, a direct evolution of the Lotus 7 designed by the legendary Colin Chapman. Although the original became something of cult vehicle following its appearance in the *The Prisoner* television series of the 1960s, Lotus ceased production of the kit-car in 1972. Caterham bought up the rights and continue to offer its derivatives in both kit-car and fully assembled form. *(JC)*

Reading, Guildford, and Reigate Branch

This line connects the county towns of Berkshire and Surrey (Reading: and Guildford), and extends from the latter across the garden of Surrey to Reigate; at the same time communicating with four trunk lines – the Great Western, the South Western, the Brighton, and the South Eastern Railway. To the pleasure tourist we scarcely know any presenting so many picturesque attractions. Its route lies from Reading along the South Eastern line, across Berkshire, by Wokingham and Sandhurst, entering Surrey by Tinley; then crossing the South Western line, onward with a branch to Farnham; at the base of Hog's Back to Guildford; next by a branch to Godalming, and continuing at the foot of the celebrated range of chalk hills past Dorking and Reigate to Red Hill. We have alluded to the picturesqueness of the Surrey portion, which will be new ground to many a tourist; though it is perhaps, the most beautiful scenery of its class in England. Its landscapes present a rich succession of 'morceaux' for the painter in its picturesque uplands, woodland, dells, verdant valleys, rocky hills and undulating parks and heaths, all lying within the eye of the traveller along this line. Betchworth Park is among the most beautiful specimens of this scenery between Reigate and Dorking, although the part of the chalk hills seen from that point is greatly exceeded by the bolder sublimity of Box Hill, the venerable giant of the chain, with its luxuriant clothing of patronymic evergreen.

As a pleasure line, tills portion is very popular, passing as it does through an exceedingly fine country, with the scenery of which excursion trains have already made thousands of visitors familiar.

[Bradshaw's description starts at Reigate with the line going to the west.]

BETCHWORTH

A telegraph station.

Within a short distance, situated most beautifully in a romantic park washed by the 'Sullen Mole', are the ruins of Betchworth Castle.

They are most picturesque, and the grey walls, contrasting with the rich green of the ivy creeping over a great part of them, stand out finely against the deep blue sky.

Proceeding on our way, with the lofty down on our right, we pass over the Mole by a viaduct 50 feet high, and then through Box Tunnel to the station at

BOX HILL

A telegraph station.

Tourists alight at this station for the hill with its celebrated prospects. It took its name from the Box trees planted thereon in tire reign of Charles I and is now a resort for pic-nic parties.

This is the nearest station likewise for Mickleham, a charming village, 2 1/2 miles distant.

Boxhill/Dorking

Left: Broadwood's Folly, Box Hill. Built by Thomas Broadwood, owner of Juniper Hall, Mickleham, in around 1820. The Bradshaw Guide describes Mickleham as a 'charming' village. *(Mertbiol)*

Below: Renamed Deepdene in 1923, to avoid confusion with Box Hill and Westhumble station on the Horsham-Sutton line and Dorking (Deepdene) in May 1987, this is the principle station on the Reading–Redhill line in Dorking and, despite its minimal facilities is very busy with commuting schoolchildren. The South Eastern Railway tried to promote it as the railhead for Box Hill, although the other Box Hill and Westhumble is far closer to that noted beauty spot. *(Michael Fife)*

Dorking itself, like Reigate, is now a commuter town but is blessed by being surrounded by the Surrey Hills Area of Outstanding Natural Beauty. Just north-east of the town the River Mole cuts a steep-sided valley through the North Downs. On the left bank is Denbies Vineyard, the largest in the UK and on the right, Box Hill, owned by the National Trust. To the south west of the town is Leith Hill which, with its tower, climbs to 1,000 feet above sea level.

Hotels – Running Horse, Fox and Hounds.

Norbury Park (2 ½ miles), H. P. Spirling, Esq. A beautiful seat surrounded by fine plantations. One mile beyond this is the town of Leatherhead, see page 75.

DORKING

Population, 4,161. Distance from the station, ½ mile,

A telegraph station. Red Hotels – Red Lion, and White Horse.

Omnibuses to and from the station; to Epsom station several times daily; to Brighton and London thrice weekly. Market Day – Thursday. Fair – The day before Holy Thursday. Money Order Office. Bankers – London and County Joint Stock Banking Company.

Dorking is situated in a valley near the river Mole, nearly surrounded with hills, and commands some of the finest views in the kingdom. This town is of considerable antiquity, and so conveniently situated that it carries on a large trade in flour and corn, and employs several mills on the Mole. The church is a fine old edifice and contains several handsome monuments. It is celebrated for its poultry, particularly for a five-toed breed, called Dorkings, supposed to have been introduced by the Romans. It is a favourite summer resort of invalids and lovers of rural scenery, and it would be difficult to name any place better calculated for both classes, as the salubrity of the air and the beauty of the surrounding country cannot be surpassed or equalled within so short a distance of the metropolis. There are several very beautiful country-seats, villas, and mansions around the town, too numerous, however, to be enumerated in our pages.

The line, still skirting the Downs, soon brings us to the station of

GOMSHALL AND SHEIRE

A telegraph station.

Sheire was the residence of Bray, the antiquarian, who edited Evelyn's Memoirs. In the immediate vicinity is *Abinger Hall* (2 miles), the seat of Lord Abinger. *Netley Place* (1 ½ mile). *Albury Park* (1 ½ mile). Near which is Newland's Corner, from which a most extensive prospect may be obtained.

East Horsley (3 miles). *Ewhurst* (5 miles).

CHILWORTH

Distance from station, 1 mile. A telegraph station.

On an eminence in the vicinity, and towards the south, is St Martha's ancient chapel *Chilworth Manor* is the property of Godwin Austin, Esq.

About two miles further is ...

Guildford

The county town of Surrey, home to a castle, the University of Surrey and an Anglican cathedral, shown left. It is of Saxon origin, probably located where the River Wey was forded by the Harrow Way. On the building of the Wey Navigation and Basingstoke Canal, Guildford was connected to a network of waterways that aided its prosperity.

Below: The station was opened by the London & South Western Railway on 5 May 1845, but was substantially enlarged and rebuilt in 1880. The RGRR arrived on 4 July 1849, while services to Farnham in October 1849, to Horsham in October 1865 and the New Guildford Line to Leatherhead and Epsom Downs in February 1885 completed the railway map. Although modernised by British Rail, the station is a rather untidy, unattractive affair and could do with a complete rebuild. *(Simon Jeffs)*

SHALFORD

Distance from station, 1/2 mile. A telegraph station.

Mails – One arrival and departure, daily, between London and Shalford.

Money Order at Guildford.

Half a mile from the station is the village, near which is *Shalford House*, the demesne of Sir Henry Austin, whose mansion is embellished with some fine specimens of carved wood, and a collection of good paintings by the old masters.

GUILDFORD

A Population, 8,020. A telegraph station. Hotels – White Lion and White Hart.

Omnibuses to and from the station. Post Horses, Flys, etc., at the station and hotels.

Carriers to London (twice weekly); also to Ash, Albury, Alford, Loxwood, Rudgwick, Bookham, Effingham, Bisley, Knaphill, Bramlcy, Chichester, Midhurst, Haslemere, Chiddingfold, Cranley, Dunsfold, Ewhurst, Frimley, Godalming, Huscomb, Horshell, Woking, Kidford, Chobham, Liphook, Petersfield, Petworth. Pulborough, Ripley, Send, Sheire, Wisborough Green, Wonersh, Worplesdon, Pirbright.

Market Days – Saturday, Tuesday & Wednesday. Fairs – May 4th and November 22nd. Money Order Office.

The situation of this town on the banks of the Wey, and spreading over the steep hill as it rises from the side of the river, is particularly picturesque. It consists of a principal street, nearly a mile long from the bridge on the west to Stoke on the east, whence, several smaller streets extend into the suburbs.

Guildford Castle is supposed to have been built as early as the time of the Anglo-Saxon kings. The principal part now remaining is the keep, of a quadrangular form, rising to the height of 70 feet, and built on an artificial mound of earth. Admission may be had free on application to the proprietor of a school adjoining the castle grounds.

Two miles to the eastward of the town is a fine circular race-course. The roads in the neighbourhood are extremely picturesque – that from Guildford to Farnham in particular, running along a ridge of high chalk hills, and thus commanding an extensive prospect. The trade of the town is considerable, from its central situation and convenient distance from the metropolis. The guild or town-hall and the corn market are handsome buildings.

ASH

Distance from the station, 1/4 mile. A telegraph station.

Omnibuses to and from the station; also to the Farnham station.

Money Order Office at Famham.

[The line then diverges or turns more towards the north, across the county border to Aldershot.]

Crawley to Petworth

Crawley, at about the midway point on the London to Brighton road, has been a market town since the thirteenth century, but expanded massively in the 1950s to become one of the New Towns ringing London. The station was opened with the line from Three Bridges to Horsham in 1848, but was too small to cope with the rising population of the New Town and was replaced in July 1968 by a new, larger structure just to the east of the old facility, shown top left.

Horsham was an important commercial centre and has been known for horse trading, iron, brick-making, and brewing more recently. Horsham grew up around the Carfax, a meeting place of four roads, while to the south of the Carfax is the Causeway. This tranquil street consists of houses erected in the seventeenth–nineteenth centuries and is lined with ancient London Plane trees. At its south end is the parish church of St Mary, shown left. The current Grade II station is pure Southern Railway, being totally rebuilt in the 'International Modern' style, complete with nearby 'Odeon' signal box, when the Portsmouth–Bognor line was electrified in 1938. *(Michael Fife)*

Below: Petworth House, with park by Capability Brown. Now owned by the National Trust. *(Laurel Arnison)*

Sussex Branch Lines

Horsham Branch

THREE BRIDGES TO HORSHAM AND PETWORTH

This branch is 8½ miles in length. From Three Bridges the line proceeds nearly in a west-south-west direction to the station at

CRAWLEY

A neat, clean town, of some note in the coaching times.

The line passes through a rural district, presenting no feature of importance, to

FAY GATE

In the vicinity of Lord St Leonard's estate. Money Order Office.

A telegraph station.

HORSHAM

A Population, 6,747. A telegraph station. Hotels – King's Head, and Anchor.

Market Days – Saturdays (corn), Mondays (poultry). Fairs – April 5th and 18th, July 17th, November 27th, and Monday before Whitsuntide.

This town stands on the River Adur, and is considered, in a commercial point of view, one of the most important in the county.

Billingshurst and Pulborough Stations.

PETWORTH

A telegraph station. Hotels – The Swan; Half Moon.

This town has a population of 2,326, and occupies a very healthy situation near the river Rother. The principal attraction is *Petworth House*, close by, the superb residence of general Wyndham, formerly that of the Earls of Northumberland. Here are a fine collection of paintings, many by Vandyke, old tapestry and various works of art, together with the sword used by Hotspur at the battle of Shrewsbury. The park, in which the museum stands, is 12 miles in circumference. In the church may be seen many of the tombs of the Perceys and Wyndhams.

Continuing our route from Horsham, we pass the stations of Southwater, West Grinstead, Partridge Green, and Henfield, to the small town of ...

Above left: Bramber Castle. *(Laurel Arnison)*

East Grinstead

The town is close to Ashdown Forest where the Winnie the Pooh stories are set, and is also the site of Queen Victoria Hospital, where plastic surgeon Archibald McIndoe treated burns victims of the Second World War in the 'Guinea Pig Club'. East Grinstead was reached by the railway from Three Bridges in 1848, but the only link to the national rail system is through Oxted to South Croydon, which was not opened until 1884. A new station building, upper left, opened in 2013. *(Stuart Hicks)* That same year, the Bluebell Railway finally reached the town, shown above, from Sheffield Park, after a heroic effort. *(Simon Jeffs)*

Lewes

The county town of East Sussex and historically of all of Sussex. *Left:* The 1888 station. *Lower left:* The castle, built by the Saxons and rebuilt by the Normans. *Below:* Harvey's Brewery dominates the lower part of the town. *(Simon Jeffs)*

STEYNING

A telegraph station. Market Day – Wednesday.

Fairs – June 9th, September 20th, and October 10th.

This place stands on the river Adur, at the foot of a hill. It enjoyed the privileges of a borough by prescriptive right, and returned two members to parliament up to the passing of the Reform Bill, by which it was disfranchised.

BRAMBER

Disfranchised by the Reform Bill; a place of no particular interest beyond the remains of a castle, which dates from about the time of the Conquest.

East Grinstead Branch

THREE BRIDGES TO EAST GRINSTEAD

This branch is about 6½ miles long, passing through the small village of Rowfant, four miles beyond which brings us to the town of

EAST GRINSTEAD

A telegraph station. Market Day – Thursday. Fairs – Last Thurs. in every month; also April 21st, June 25th, November 8th, and December 11th.

This was one of the places disfranchised by the Reform Act of 1832. It contains a population of 4,266, and a good sized church with a monument, the inscription on which purports the church to have been founded by R. Lewkner Esq., the wife of whom had been connected with the courts of Edward IV and Henry VII.

Newhaven Branch

HAYWARD'S HEATH TO LEWES AND NEWHAVEN

The line passes through an undulating, and in some places a hilly, country, to Cook's Bridge. Three miles farther the train reaches

LEWES

Population, 9,716. Distance from station, ½ mile. A telegraph station.

Hotels – White Hart, family; Crown, commercial.

Market Day – Tuesday. Fairs – Whit Tuesday, May 6th. July 26th, and Sept. 21st.

Lewes is a borough town in the county of Sussex, and one of the largest and most important in the whole county. It stands on the banks of the River Ouse, about seven miles from the sea-coast. Lewes is a place of great antiquity, and the vestiges of walls

Left: Isfield station is on the line reopened as the Lavender Line heritage railway. This is open most weekends from Easter to October, operating a variety of steam and diesel traction. *(Simon Jeffs)*

Newhaven

The village was of little maritime importance until the opening of the railway to Lewes in 1847. The LBSCR developed the harbour between 1850 and 1878 to enable it to be used by cross channel ferries, and in 1863 the LBSCR and the Chemin de Fer de l'Ouest introduced the Newhaven–Dieppe passenger service which continues to this day, shown left. *(Simon Jeffs)* Newhaven harbour was designated as the principal port for the movement of men and materiel to the Continent during the First World War and was taken over by the military authorities with the ferries requisitioned for the duration. Newhaven has three railway stations, Town, Harbour and Marine, the last of which used to be used by boat trains but is now mothballed due to the downturn in foot passengers on the ferries. *Below:* The Newhaven boat train in 1925. *(B. J. Holden)*

and entrenchments still remaining prove how strong the fortifications must have been. It is well built, and contains several excellent streets, with uniform and elegant buildings. There are also two large suburbs, one on the west side of the town called Southover, and the other on the east side of the river, on a chalk cliff, and hence called Cliff. It contains seven churches, and the ruins of an old castle, and will be memorable in future ages as having been the abode of the Russian prisoners captured by the Allied Powers of England and France in the fierce contests of 1854–55.

Uckfield Branch

LEWES TO UCKFIELD

From hence this line, 7 miles long, passes through the villages of Barcombe and Isfield to

UCKFIELD

A telegraph station. Hotels – Maidenhead; Bell.

Besides its two chalybeate springs in the neighbourhood it has no particular attractions.

NEWHAVEN

A telegraph station Hotel – Bridge Inn.
Steam Packets to Dieppe daily in summer, to Jersey, twice weekly. Fair – October 16th.

Newhaven, formerly a very obscure port or fishing town at the month of the river Ouse, is now a rising place, and become of some importance, as the port of communication between London, Dieppe, and Paris. Louis Philippe landed here in 1818, after his flight from France.

[On the eastern side of Sussex the railway from Kent enters the county via two lines – Tunbridge Wells to St Leonards, and from Ashford to Rye and Winchelsea. The Kent sections are described in full in *Bradshaw's Guide 4: South Eastern Railways*, also published by Amberley.]

TUNBRIDGE WELLS TO ST LEONARDS

From Tunbridge Wells the railway proceeds southward, and enters the county of Sussex, passing through a short tunnel at starting, and then proceeds through a deep cutting ...

FRANT

Distance from station, 1 mile. A telegraph station. Hotels – Spread Eagle, and Abergavenny Arms. Money Order Office at Tunbridge Wells.

A short distance from this station is Eridge Castle, the demesne of the Earl of Abergavenny, situated in a noble park, well stocked with deer. There are several handsome villas in the neighbourhood, the scenery of which is exceedingly varied, and some of the views of the country around are both extensive and beautiful.

Between Frant and Robertsbridge the scenery becomes less picturesque, though the country is highly cultivated, and the hop-grounds are particularly fine. Near the Wadhurst station there is rather a long tunnel, and the church of Wadhurst is worthy a visit.

WADHURST

Distance from station, 1 mile. A telegraph station. Market Day – Saturday. Fairs – April 29th and November 1st. Money Order Office at Wadhurst.

TICEHURST ROAD

Distance from station, 1 mile. A telegraph station. Market Day – Sat. Fairs – May 4, and Oct. 7. Money Order Office at Ticehurst.

The Battle line
William the Conqueror erected the abbey at Battle, above left, to commemorate his victory and the town has grown up around it. It remains a tourist magnet, patronage increasing when the SER extended its line from Tunbridge Wells. *(Laurel Arnison)*

Left: The station at Frant. *(Simon Jeffs)*

Above: Batemans, on the road from Etchingham to Burwash, was the home of Rudyard Kipling. *(Simon Jeffs)*

Ticehurst is rather a large town, situated on high ground, about three miles and a half to the east of the station, in the midst of a splendid agricultural country.

ETCHINGHAM

Distance from station, 1 mile. A telegraph station. Money Order Office at Wadhurst.

The church at Etchingham is a fine old edifice, reputed to be one of the best specimens of Norman architecture in the country.

The stations at Front, Etchinghnm, and Battle are built in the Gothic character; those at Wadhurst, Ticehurst Bead, and Robertsbridge are in the Italian style, of red and white brick and Caen stone.

ROBERTSBRIDGE

Distance from station, ¼ mile. A telegraph station. Hotel – Old George.

Market Day – Thursday. Money Order Office at Robertabridge.

The village is situated on the banks of the river Bother, and only remarkable for the houses being constructed of red brick, which gives the place a peculiar appearance.

BATTLE

Distance from station, 1 mile. A telegraph station. Hotel – George. Omnibuses to and from the station. Post Horses, Flys, etc., at the hotel. Market Day – The second Monday in each month. Fairs – Whit Monday and November 22nd.

This town was formerly called Epiton, and received its present name from being the spot on which the Saxons, under Harold, wore defeated by William, the Duke of Normandy, in 1006. After the contest the Conqueror founded a magnificent abbey to commemorate his victory, and the high altar in the church is said to have stood on the very spot where the body of the heroic Saxon prince was found. The noble gateway of the abbey has a fine effect when seen from the town. In the abbey was formerly preserved the celebrated Battle Abbey Roll, which formed a list of those families which came over from Normandy with the Duke.

The mingled scene of hill and dale, wood and village, presents one of those fair spots in nature which refresh the traveller, who, hurrying through tunnel and cutting, to annihilate time and space, too often disregards the beauty of the country through which he passes.

Four miles further is

ST LEONARDS STATION

[See page 57 for description. Hastings – see page 59.]

ROSE GARDEN, ROYAL ALBION HOTEL
BRIGHTON

Postcard of Brighton's Royal Albion. *(CMcC)*

Acknowledgements

Thanks go the following sources for providing additional images for this book: Campbell McCutcheon *(CMcC)*, US Library of Congress *(LoC)*, Tony Hisgett, John Scrace, Graham Feakins, Colin Scott-Morton, Laurel Arnison, Michael Baker, Gregg M. Erickson, Stuart Hicks, Darren, Peter Castleton, Lester Hayes, Poliphilo, Fred Matthews, Jim, Belchingmatt, Mertbiol, Jeanhousen, Michael Fife, B. J. Holden and the SEG archives.

Front cover: *Glynde* locomotive, Tony Hisgett. Brighton's Palace Pier in 2007, Jeanhousen. Back cover: Campbell McCutcheon and Simon Jeffs.